THE TRIALS O
BROTHER JER
AND
THE STRONG

TWO PLAYS BY
WOLE SOYINKA

★

DRAMATISTS
PLAY SERVICE
INC.

THE TRIALS OF BROTHER JERO and THE STRONG BREED
were first presented by Farris-Belgrave Productions in association with
Afolabi Ajayi at the Greenwich Mews Theatre, in New York City,
on November 9, 1967. They were directed by Cynthia Belgrave; the
sets and lighting were by Jack Blackman; original costumes from
Nigeria were by Edward Wolrond; music composed and arranged by
Pat Patrick. The cast, in order of appearance, was as follows:

THE TRIALS OF BROTHER JERO

BROTHER JERO, *a beach divine* .... Harold Scott
OLD PROPHET, *his mentor* .... Dennis Tate
CHUME, *assistant to Jero* .... Afolabi Ajayi
AMOPE, *his wife* .... Cynthia Belgrave
A TRADER WOMAN .... Peggy Kirkpatrick
GIRL, *who passes by* .... Lauren Jones
DRUMMER BOY .... Edward Luis Espinosa
PENITENT .... Yvonne Worden
MEMBER OF PARLIAMENT .... Roger Robinson
NEIGHBOURS, VILLAGERS AND WORSHIPPERS .... Yvette Hawkins,
G. Tito Shaw, Mary Alice, Vernon Washington, James Spruill

THE STRONG BREED

EMAN, *a stranger* .... Harold Scott
SUNMA, *Jaguna's daughter* .... Mary Alice
IFADA, *an idiot* .... Edward Luis Espinosa
A SICK GIRL .... Yvette Hawkins
JAGUNA .... James Spruill
OROGE .... Dennis Tate
ATTENDANT STALWARTS AND VILLAGERS .... Peggy Kirkpatrick,
Afolabi Ajayi, Yvonne Worden,
Tom Hawkins, Austin Briggs Hall, Jr.

(From Eman's Past)

EMAN'S FATHER .... Robertearl Jones
ATTENDANT .... Willie Woods
OMAE, *young Eman's betrothed* .... Lauren Jones
YOUNG EMAN .... G. Tito Shaw
TUTOR .... Vernon Washington
PRIEST .... Roger Robinson

3

The Trials of Brother Jero

A Play by Wole Soyinka

CAST OF CHARACTERS

JEROBOAM, *a beach divine*

OLD PROPHET, *his mentor*

CHUME, *assistant to Jeroboam*

AMOPE, *his wife*

A TRADER

MEMBER OF PARLIAMENT

PENITENT

NEIGHBOURS

WORSHIPPERS

A TOUCH MAMMA

A YOUNG GIRL

The Trials of Brother Jero

SCENE 1

The stage is completely dark. A spotlight reveals the Prophet, a heavily but neatly bearded man; his hair is thick and high, but well-combed, unlike that of most prophets. Suave is the word for him. He carries a canvas pouch and a divine rod.* He speaks directly and with his accustomed loftiness to the audience.

JERO. I am a prophet. A prophet by birth and by inclination. You have probably seen many of us on the streets, many with their own churches, many inland, many on the coast, many leading processions, many looking for processions to lead, many curing the deaf, many raising the dead. In fact, there are eggs and there are eggs. Same thing with prophets.

I was born a prophet. I think my parents found that I was born with rather thick and long hair. It was said to come right down to my eyes and down to my neck. For them, this was a certain sign that I was born a natural prophet.

And I grew to love the trade. It used to be a very respectable one in those days and competition was dignified. But in the last few years, the beach has become fashionable, and the struggle for land has turned the profession into a thing of ridicule. Some prophets I could name gained their present beaches by getting women penitents to shake their bosoms in spiritual ecstasy. This prejudiced the councillors who came to divide the beach among us.

Yes, it did come to the point where it became necessary for the Town Council to come to the beach and settle the prophets' territorial warfare once and for all. My master, the same one who brought me up in prophetic ways, staked his claim and won a grant of land. . . . I helped him, with a campaign led by six dancing girls from the French territory, all dressed as Jehovah's Witnesses.

* A metal rod about 15" long, tapered, bent into a ring at the thick end.

What my old master did not realize was that I was really helping myself.

Mind you, the beach is hardly worth having these days. The worshippers have dwindled to a mere trickle and we really have to fight for every new convert. They all prefer high life to the rhythm of celestial hymns. And television too is keeping our wealthier patrons at home. They used to come in the evening when they would not easily be recognized. Now they stay at home and watch television. However, my whole purpose in coming here is to show you one rather eventful day in my life, a day when I thought for a moment that the curse of my old master was about to be fulfilled. It shook me quite a bit, but . . . the Lord protects his own. . . .

(Enter old prophet shaking his fist.)

OLD PROPHET. Ungrateful wretch! Is this how you repay the long years of training I have given you? To drive me, your old tutor, off my piece of land . . . telling me I have living beyond my time. Ha! May you be rewarded in the same manner. May the wheel come right round and find you just as helpless as you make me now. . . . (He continues to mouth curses, but inaudibly.)

JERO. (Ignoring him.) He didn't move me one bit. The old dodderer had been foolish enough to imagine that when I organised the campaign to acquire his land in competition with (Ticking them off on his fingers.) —The Brotherhood of Jero, the Cherubims and Seraphims, the Sisters of Judgement Day, the Heavenly Cowboys, not to mention the Jehovah's Witnesses whom the French girls impersonated—, well, he must have been pretty conceited to think that I did it all for him.

OLD PROPHET. Ingrate! Monster! I curse you with the curse of the daughters of discord. May they be your downfall. May the daughters of Eve bring ruin down on your head! (Old Prophet goes off, shaking his fist.)

JERO. Actually that was a very cheap curse. He knew very well that I had one weakness—women. Not my fault, mind you. You must admit that I am rather good-looking . . . no, don't be misled, I am not at all vain. Nevertheless, I decided to be on my guard. The call of prophecy is in my blood and I would not risk my calling with the fickleness of women. So I kept away from them. I am still single and since that day when I came into my own, no scandal has ever touched my name. And it was a sad day indeed when I woke up one morning and the first thing to meet my eyes was a daughter of Eve. You may compare that feeling with waking up and finding a vulture crouched on your bed post.

BLACKOUT

SCENE 2

Early morning.
A few poles with nets and other litter denote a fishing village. D. R. *is the corner of a hut, window on one side, door on the other.*
A cycle bell is heard ringing. Seconds after, a cycle is ridden on stage towards the hut. The rider is a shortish man; his feet barely touch the pedals. On the cross-bar is a woman; the cross-bar itself is wound round with a mat, and on the carrier is a large travelling sack, with a short woman's stool hanging from a corner of it.

AMOPE. Stop here. Stop here. That's his house. (*The man applies the brakes too suddenly. The weight leans towards the woman's side, with the result that she props up the bicycle with her feet, rather jerkily. It is in fact no worse than any ordinary landing, but it is enough to bring out her sense of aggrievement. When she speaks, her tone of martyrdom is easy, accustomed to use.*) I suppose we all do our best, but after all these years one would think you could set me down a little more gently.

CHUME. You didn't give me much notice. I had to brake suddenly.

AMOPE. The way you complain—anybody who didn't see what happened would think you were the one who broke an ankle. (*She has already begun to limp.*)

CHUME. Don't tell me that was enough to break your ankle.

AMOPE. Break? You didn't hear me complain. You did your best, but if my toes are to be broken one by one just because I have to monkey on your bicycle, you must admit it's a tough life for a woman.

CHUME. I did my. . . .

AMOPE. Yes, you did your best. I know. Didn't I admit it? Please . . . give me that stool. . . . You know yourself that I'm not the one to make much of a little thing like that, but I haven't been too

9

well. If anyone knows that, it's you. Thank you (*Taking the stool.*) . . . I haven't been well, that's all, otherwise I wouldn't have said a thing. (*She sits down near the door of the hut, sighing heavily, and begins to nurse her feet.*)

CHUME. Do you want me to bandage it for you?

AMOPE. No, no. What for? (*Chume hesitates, then begins to unload the bundle.*)

CHUME. You're sure you don't want me to take you back? If it swells after I've gone . . .

AMOPE. I can look after myself. I've always done, and looked after you too. Just help me to unload the things and place them against the wall . . . you know I wouldn't ask if it wasn't for the ankle. (*Chume had placed the bag next to her, thinking that was all. He returns now to untie the bundle. Brings out a small brazier covered with paper which is tied down, two small saucepans.*) You haven't let the soup pour out, have you?

CHUME. (*With some show of exasperation.*) Do you see oil on the wrapper? (*Throws down the wrapper.*)

AMOPE. Abuse me. All right, go on, begin to abuse me. You know that all I asked was if the soup had poured away, and it isn't as if that was something no one ever asked before. I would do it all myself if it wasn't for my ankle—anyone would think it was my fault . . . careful . . . careful now . . . the cork nearly came off that bottle. You know how difficult it is to get any clean water in this place. . . . (*Chume unloads two bottles filled with water, two little parcels wrapped in paper, another tied in a knot, a box of matches, a piece of yam, two tins, one probably an Ovaltine tin but contains something else of course, a cheap breakable spoon, a knife, while Amope keeps up her patient monologue, spoken almost with indifference.*) Do, I beg you, take better care of that jar . . . I know you didn't want to bring me, but it wasn't the fault of the jar, was it?

CHUME. Who said I didn't want to bring you?

AMOPE. You said it was too far away for you to bring me on your bicycle . . . I suppose you really wanted me to walk. . . .

CHUME. I. . . .

AMOPE. And after you'd broken my foot, the first thing you asked was if you should take me home. You were only too glad it happened . . . in fact if I wasn't the kind of person who would never think evil of anyone—even you—I would have said that you did it on purpose. (*The unloading is over. Chume shakes out the bag.*) Just leave the bag here. I can use it for a pillow.

CHUME. Is there anything else before I go?

AMOPE. You've forgotten the mat. I know it's not much, but I would like something to sleep on. There are women who sleep in beds of course, but I'm not complaining. They are just lucky with their husbands, and we can't all be lucky, I suppose.

CHUME. You've got a bed at home. (*He unties the mat which is wound round the cross-bar.*)

AMOPE. And so I'm to leave my work undone. My trade is to suffer because I have a bed at home? Thank God I am not the kind of woman who. . . .

CHUME. I am nearly late for work.

AMOPE. I know you can't wait to get away. You only use your work as an excuse. A Chief Messenger in the Local Government Office—do you call that work? Your old school friends are now Ministers, riding in long cars. . . . (*Chume gets on his bike and flees. Amope shouts after him, craning her neck in his direction.*) Don't forget to bring some more water when you're returning from work. (*She relapses and sighs heavily.*) He doesn't realise it is all for his own good. He's no worse than other men, but he won't make the effort to become something in life. A Chief Messenger. Am I to go to my grave as the wife of a Chief Messenger? (*She is seated so that the prophet does not immediately see her when he opens the window to breathe some fresh air. He stares straight out for a few moments, then shuts his eyes tightly, clasps his hands together above his chest, chin uplifted for a few moments' meditation. He relaxes and is about to go in when he sees Amope's back. He leans out to try and take in the rest of her but this proves impossible. Puzzled, he leaves the window and goes round to the door which is then seen to open about a foot and shut rapidly. Amope is calmly chewing cola. As the door shuts she takes out a notebook and a pencil and checks some figures, Brother Jeroboam, known to his congregation as Brother Jero, is seen again at the window, this time with his canvas pouch and divine stick. He lowers the bag to the ground, eases one leg over the window. Amope, without looking back.*) Where do you think you're going? (*Brother Jero practically flings himself back into the house.*) One pound, eight shillings and ninepence for three months. And he calls himself a man of God. (*She puts the notebook away, unwraps the brazier and pro-*

11

ceeds to light it preparatory to getting breakfast. The door opens another foot.)

JERO. (*Coughs.*) Sister . . . my dear sister in Christ. . . .

AMOPE. I hope you slept well, Brother Jero. . . .

JERO. Yes, thanks be to God. (*Hems and coughs.*) I—er—I hope you have not come to stand in the way of Christ and his work.

AMOPE. If Christ doesn't stand in the way of me and my work.

JERO. Beware of pride, sister. That was a sinful way to talk.

AMOPE. Listen, you bearded debtor. You owe me one pound, eight and nine. You promised you would pay me three months ago but of course you have been too busy doing the work of God. Well, let me tell you that you are not going anywhere until you do a bit of my own work.

JERO. But the money is not in the house. I must get it from the post office before I can pay you.

AMOPE. (*Fanning the brazier.*) You'll have to think of something else before you call me a fool. (*Brother Jeroboam shuts the door. A woman trader goes past with a deep calabash bowl on her head.*) Ei, what are you selling? (*The trader hesitates, decides to continue on her way.*) Isn't it you I'm calling? What have you got there?

TRADER. (*Stops, without turning round.*) Are you buying for trade or just for yourself?

AMOPE. It might help if you first told me what you have.

TRADER. Smoked fish.

AMOPE. Well, let's see it.

TRADER. (*Hesitates.*) All right, help me to set it down. But I don't usually stop on the way.

AMOPE. Isn't it money you are going to the market for, and isn't it money I'm going to pay you?

TRADER. (*As Amope gets up and unloads her.*) Well, just remember it is early in the morning. Don't start me off wrong by haggling.

AMOPE. All right, all right. (*Looks at the fish.*) How much a dozen?

TRADER. One and three, and I'm not taking a penny less.

AMOPE. It is last week's, isn't it?

TRADER. I've told you, you're my first customer, so don't ruin my trade with the ill-luck of the morning.

AMOPE. (*Holding one up to her nose.*) Well, it does smell a bit, doesn't it?

TRADER. (*Putting back the wrappings.*) Maybe it is you who haven't had a bath for a week.

AMOPE. Yeh! All right, go on. Abuse me. Go on and abuse me when all I wanted was a few of your miserable fish. I deserve it for trying to be neighbourly with a cross-eyed wretch, pauper that you are. . . .

TRADER. It is early in the morning. I am not going to let you infect my luck with your foul tongue by answering you back. And just you keep your cursed fingers from my goods because that is where you'll meet with the father of all devils if you don't. (*She lifts the load to her head all by herself.*)

AMOPE. Yes, go on. Carry the burden of your crimes and take your beggar's rags out of my sight. . . .

TRADER. I leave you in the hands of your flatulent belly, you barren sinner. May you never do good in all your life.

AMOPE. You're cursing me now, are you? (*She leaps up just in time to see Brother Jero escape through the window.*) Help! Thief! Thief! You bearded rogue. Call yourself a prophet? But you'll find it is easier to get out than to get in. You'll find that out or my name isn't Amope. . . . (*She turns on the trader who has already disappeared.*) Do you see what you have done, you spindle-leg toad? Receiver of stolen goods, just wait until the police catch up with you. . . . (*Towards the end of this speech the sound of gan-gan drums is heard, coming from the side opposite the hut. A boy enters carrying a drum on each shoulder. He walks towards her, drumming. She turns almost at once.*) Take yourself off, you dirty beggar. Do you think my money is for the likes of you? (*The boy flees, turns suddenly and beats a parting abuse on the drums.**) I don't know what the world is coming to. A thief of a prophet, a swindler of a fish-seller and now that thing with lice on his head comes begging for money. He and that prophet ought to get to-gether. Wouldn't surprise me in fact if they were father and son.

LIGHTS FADE

---

* Urchins often go through the streets with a drum, begging for alms. But their skill is used also for insults even without provocation.

*A short while later. The beach. A few stakes and palm
leaves denote the territory of Brother Jeroboam's church.
To one side is a palm tree, and in the center is a heap of
sand with assorted empty bottles, a small mirror, and
hanging from one of the bottles is a rosary and cross.
Brother Jero is standing as he was last seen when he made
his escape—white flowing gown and a very fine velvet
white also. He stands upright, divine rod in one hand,
while the other caresses the velvet cape.*

JERO. I don't know how she found out my house. When I bought
the goods off her, she did not even ask any questions. My calling
was enough to guarantee payment. It is not as if this was a well
paid job. And it is not what I would call a luxury, this velvet cape
which I bought from her. It would not have been necessary if one
were not forced to distinguish himself more and more from these
scum who degrade the calling of the prophet. It becomes important
to stand out, to be distinctive. I have set my heart after a particular name. They will look at my velvet cape and they will think of
my goodness. Inevitably they must begin to call me . . . the vel-
vet-hearted Jeroboam. (*Straightens himself.*) Immaculate Jero,
Articulate Hero of Christ's Crusade. . . . Well, it is out. I have
not breathed it to a single soul, but that has been my ambition.
You've got to have a name that appeals to the imagination—because the imagination is a thing of the spirit—it must catch the
imagination of the crowd. Yes, one must move with modern times.
Lack of colour gets one nowhere even in the prophet's business.
(*Looks all round him.*) Charlatans! If only I had this beach to myself. (*With sudden violence.*) But how does one maintain his
dignity when the daughter of Eve forces him to leave his own house
through a window? God curse that woman! I never thought she
would dare affront the presence of a man of God. One pound eight
for this little cape. It is sheer robbery. (*He surveys the scene again.
A young girl passes, sleepily, clothed only in her wrapper.*) She
passes here every morning, on her way to take a swim. Dirty-
looking thing. (*He yawns.*) I am glad I got here before any customers—I mean worshippers—well, customers if you like. I always
get that feeling every morning that I am a shop-keeper waiting for

14

customers. The regular ones come at definite times. Strange, dissatisfied people. I know they are dissatisfied because I keep them dissatisfied. Once they are full, they won't come again. Like my good apprentice, Brother Chume. He wants to beat his wife, but I won't let him. If I do, he will become contented, and then that's another of my flock gone for ever. As long as he doesn't beat her, he comes here feeling helpless, and so there is no chance of his rebelling against me. Everything, in fact, is planned. (*The young girl crosses the stage again. She has just had her swim and the difference is remarkable. Clean, wet, shiny face and hair. She continues to wipe herself with her wrapper as she walks. Jero follows her all the way with his eyes.*) Every morning, every day I witness this divine transformation, O Lord. (*He shakes his head suddenly and bellows.*) Pray Brother Jeroboam, pray! Pray for strength against temptation. (*He falls on his knees, face squeezed in agony and hands clasped. Chume enters, wheeling his bike. He leans it against the palm tree. Jero, not opening his eyes:*) Pray with me, brother. Pray with me. Pray for me against this one weakness . . . against this one weakness, O Lord. . . .

CHUME. (*Falling down at once.*) Help him, Lord. Help him, Lord.

JERO. Against this one weakness, this weakness, O Abraham. . . .

CHUME. Help him, Lord. Help him, Lord.

JERO. Against this one weakness David, David, Samuel, Samuel.

CHUME. Help him. Help him. Help 'am. Help 'am.

JERO. Job Job, Elijah Elijah.

CHUME. (*Getting more worked up.*) Help 'am God. Help 'am God. I say make you help 'am. Help 'am quick quick.

JERO. Tear the image from my heart. Tear this love for the daughters of Eve. . . .

CHUME. Adam, help 'am. Na your son, help 'am. Help this your son.

JERO. Burn out this lust for the daughters of Eve.

CHUME. Je-e-esu, Je-e-esu, Je-e-esu. Help 'am one time Je-e-e-su.

JERO. Abraka, Abraka, Abraka. (*Chume joins in.*) Abraka, Abraka, Hebra, Hebra, Hebra, Hebra, Hebra, Hebra, Hebra, Hebra. . . . (*Rising.*) God bless you, brother. (*Turns around.*) Chume!

CHUME. Good morning, Brother Jeroboam.

JERO. Chume, you are not at work. You've never come before in the morning.

15

CHUME. No. I went to work but I had to report sick.

JERO. Why, are you unwell, brother?

CHUME. No, Brother Jero. . . . I. . . .

JERO. A-ah, you have troubles and you could not wait to get them to God. We shall pray together.

CHUME. Brother Jero . . . I . . . I (*He stops altogether.*)

JERO. Is it difficult? Then let us commune silently for a while. (*Chume folds his arms, raises his eyes to heaven.*) I wonder what is the matter with him. Actually I knew it was he the moment he opened his mouth. Only Brother Chume reverts to that animal jabber when he gets his spiritual excitement. And that is much too often for my liking. He is too crude, but that is to my advantage. It means he would never think of setting himself up as my equal. (*He joins Chume in his meditative attitude, but almost immediately discards it, as if he has just remembered something.*) Christ my protector! It is a good job I got away from that wretched woman as soon as I did. My disciple believes that I sleep on the beach, that is, if he thinks I sleep at all. Most of them believe the same but, for myself, I prefer my bed. Much more comfortable. And it gets rather cold on the beach at nights. Still, it does them good to believe that I am something of an ascetic. . . . (*He resumes his meditative pose for a couple of moments. Gently.*) Open your mind to God, brother. This is the tabernacle of Christ. Open your mind to God. (*Chume is silent for a while then bursts out suddenly.*)

CHUME. Brother Jero, you must let me beat her!

JERO. What!

CHUME. (*Desperately.*) Just once, prophet. Just once.

JERO. Brother Chume!

CHUME. Just once. Just one sound beating, and I swear not to ask again.

JERO. Apostate. Have I not told you the will of God in this matter?

CHUME. But I've got to beat her, prophet. You must save me from madness.

JERO. I will. But only if you obey me.

CHUME. In anything else, prophet. But for this one, make you let me just beat 'am once.

JERO. Apostate!

CHUME. I no' go beat 'am too hard. Jus' once small, small.

JERO. Traitor!

16

CHUME. Jus' this one time. I no' go ask again. Jus' do me this one favour, make a beat 'am today.

JERO. Brother Chume, what were you before you came to me?

CHUME. Prophet. . . .

JERO. (Sternly.) What were you before the grace of God?

CHUME. A labourer, prophet. A common labourer.

JERO. And did I not prophesy you would become an office boy?

CHUME. You do 'am brother. Na so.

JERO. And then a messenger?

CHUME. Na you do 'am brother. Na you.

JERO. And then quick promotion? Did I not prophesy it?

CHUME. Na true, prophet. Na true.

JERO. And what are you now? What are you?

CHUME. Chief Messenger.

JERO. By the grace of God! And by the grace of God, have I not seen you at the table of the Chief Clerk? And you behind the desk, giving orders?

CHUME. Yes, prophet . . . but. . . .

JERO. With a telephone and a table bell for calling the Messenger?

CHUME. Very true, prophet, but. . . .

JERO. But? But? Kneel! (Pointing to the ground.) Kneel!

CHUME. (Wringing his hands.) Prophet!

JERO. Kneel, sinner, kneel. Hardener of heart, harbourer of Ashtoreth, protector of Baal, kneel, kneel. (Chume falls on his knees.)

CHUME. My life is a hell. . . .

JERO. Forgive him, Father, forgive him.

CHUME. This woman will kill me. . . .

JERO. Forgive him, Father, forgive him.

CHUME. Only this morning I. . . .

JERO. Forgive him, Father, forgive him.

CHUME. All the way on my bicycle. . . .

JERO. Forgive. . . .

CHUME. And not a word of thanks. . . .

JERO. Out Ashtoreth. Out Baal. . . .

CHUME. All she gave me was abuse, abuse, abuse. . . .

JERO. Hardener of the heart. . . .

CHUME. Nothing but abuse. . . .

JERO. Petrifier of the soul. . . .

CHUME. If I could only beat her once, only once. . . .

JERO. (Shouting him down.) Forgive this sinner, Father. Forgive

him by day, forgive him in the morning, forgive him at noon . . .
(*A man enters. Kneels at once and begins to chorus "Amen," or "Forgive him, Lord," or "In the name of Jesus [pronounced Je-e-e-sus]." Those who follow later do the same.*) . . . This is the son whom you appointed to follow in my footsteps. Soften his heart. Brother Chume, this woman whom you so desire to beat is your cross. Bear it well. She is your heaven-sent trial. Pray for strength and fortitude. (*Jeroboam leaves them to continue their chorus, Chume chanting "Mercy, mercy" while he makes his next remarks.*) They begin to arrive. As usual in the same order. This one who always comes earliest, I have prophesied that he will be made a chief in his home town. That is a very safe prophecy. As safe as our most popular prophecy, that a man will live to be eighty. If it doesn't come true, (*Enter an old couple, joining chorus as before.*) that man doesn't find out until he's on the other side. So everybody is quite happy. One of my most faithful adherents—unfortunately, he can only be present at week-ends—firmly believes that he is going to be the first Prime Minister of the new Mid-North-East State—when it is created. That was a risky prophecy of mine, but I badly needed more worshippers around that time. (*He looks at his watch.*) The next one to arrive is my most faithful penitent. She wants children, so she is quite a sad case. Or you would think so. But even in the midst of her most self-abasing convulsions, she manages to notice everything that goes on around her. In fact, I had better get back to the service. She is always the one to tell me that my mind is not on the service. . . . (*Altering his manner.*) Rise, Brother Chume. Rise and let the Lord enter into you. Apprentice of the Lord, are you not he upon whose shoulders my mantle must descend? (*A woman, [the penitent], enters and kneels at once in an attitude of prayer.*)

CHUME. It is so, Brother Jero.

JERO. Then why do you harden your heart? The Lord says that you may neither beat the good woman whom he has chosen to be your wife, to be your cross in your period of trial, and will you disobey him?

CHUME. No, Brother Jero.

JERO. Will you?

CHUME. No, Brother Jero.

JERO. Praise be to God.

CONGREGATION. Alleluia. (*To the clapping of hands, they*

sing a pentecostal hymn such as "I will follow Jesus," swaying and then dancing as they get warmer. Brother Jero, as the singing starts, hands two empty bottles to Chume who goes to fill them with water from the sea. Chume has hardly gone out when the drummer boy enters from u., running. He is rather weighed down by two gangan drums, and darts fearful glances back in mortal terror of whatever it is that is chasing him. This turns out, some ten or so yards later, to be a woman, sash tightened around her waist, wrapper pulled so high up that half the length of her thigh is exposed. Her sleeves are rolled above the shoulder and she is striding after the drummer in no unmistakable manner. Jeroboam, who has followed the woman's exposed limbs with quite distressed concentration, comes suddenly to himself and kneels sharply, muttering. Again the drummer appears, going across the stage in a different direction, running still. The woman follows, distance undiminished, the same set pace, Jeroboam calls to him.)

JERO. What did you do to her?

DRUMMER. *(Without stopping.)* Nothing. I was only drumming and then she said I was using it to abuse her father.

JERO. *(As the woman comes into sight.)* Woman! *(She continues out. Chume enters with filled bottles. Jero, shaking his head:)* I know her very well. She's my neighbour. But she ignored me. . . . *(Jeroboam prepares to bless the water when once again the procession appears, drummer first and the woman after.)* Come here. She wouldn't dare touch you.

DRUMMER. *(Increasing his pace.)* You don't know her. . . . *(The woman comes in sight.)*

JERO. Neighbour, neighbour. My dear sister in Moses. . . . *(She continues her pursuit offstage. Jero hesitates, then hands over his rod to Chume and goes after them.)*

CHUME. *(Suddenly remembering.)* You haven't blessed the water, Brother Jeroboam. *(Jero is already out of hearing. Chume is obviously bewildered by the new responsibility. He fiddles around with the rod and eventually uses it to conduct the singing, which has gone on all this time, flagging when the two contestants came in view, and reviving again after they had passed. Chume has hardly begun to conduct his band when a woman detaches herself from the crowd in the expected penitent's paroxysm.)*

PENITENT. Echa, echa, echa, echa, echa . . . eei, eei, eei, eei.

CHUME. *(Taken aback.)* Ngh? What's the matter?

PENITENT. Efie, efie, efie, efie, enh, enh, enh, enh. . . .

CHUME. (*Dashing off.*) Brother Jeroboam, Brother Jeroboam. . . . (*Chume shouts in all directions, returning confusedly each time in an attempt to minister to the penitent. As Jeroboam is not forthcoming, he begins, very uncertainly, to sprinkle some of the water on the penitent, crossing her on the forehead. This has to be achieved very rapidly in the brief moment when the penitent's head is lifted from being beaten on the ground. Chume, stammering:*) Father . . . forgive her.

CONGREGATION. (*Strongly.*) Amen. (*The unexpectedness of the response nearly throws Chume, but then it also serves to bolster him up, receiving such support.*)

CHUME. Father, forgive her.

CONGREGATION. Amen. (*The penitent continues to moan.*)

CHUME. Father forgive her.

CONGREGATION. Amen.

CHUME. (*Warming up to the task.*) Make you forgive 'am. Father.

CONGREGATION. Amen. (*They rapidly gain pace, Chume getting quite carried away.*)

CHUME. I say make you forgive 'am.

CONGREGATION. Amen.

CHUME. Forgive 'am one time.

CONGREGATION. Amen.

CHUME. Forgive 'am quick. Quick.

CONGREGATION. Amen.

CHUME. Forgive 'am, Father.

CONGREGATION. Amen.

CHUME. Forgive us all.

CONGREGATION. AMEN.

CHUME. Forgive us all. (*And then, punctuated regularly with Amens. . . .*) Yes, Father, make you forgive us all. Make you save us from palaver. Save us from trouble at home. Tell our wives not to give us trouble . . . (*The penitent has become placid. She is stretched out flat on the ground.*) . . . Tell our wives not to give us trouble. And give us money to have a happy home. Give us money to satisfy our daily necessities. Make you no forget those of us who dey struggle daily. Those who be clerk today, make them Chief Clerk tomorrow. Those who are Messenger today, make them Senior Service tomorrow. Yes, Father, those who are Messenger today, make them Senior Service tomorrow. (*The Amens grow more and more ecstatic.*) Those who are petty trader today, make them big contractor tomorrow. Those who dey sweep street today, give them their own big office tomorrow. If we dey walka today, give us our own bicycle tomorrow. I say those who dey walka today, give them their own bicycle tomorrow. Those who have bicycle today, they will ride their own car tomorrow. (*The enthusiasm of the response becomes, at this point, quite overpowering.*) I say those who dey push bicycle, give them big car tomorrow. Give them big car tomorrow. Give them big car tomorrow, give them big car tomorrow. (*The angry woman comes again in view, striding with the same gait as before, but now in possession of the drums. A few yards behind, the drummer jog-trots wretchedly, pleading.*)

DRUMMER. I beg you, give me my drums. I take God's name beg you, I was not abusing your father . . . for God's sake I beg you . . . I was not abusing your father. I was only drumming . . . I swear to God I was only drumming. . . . (*They pass through.*)

PENITENT. (*Who has become much alive from the latter part of the prayers, pointing. . . .*) Brother Jeroboam! (*Brother Jeroboam has just come in view. They all rush to help him back into the circle. He is a much altered man, his clothes torn and his face bleeding.*)

JERO. (*Slowly and painfully.*) Thank you, brother, sisters. Brother Chume, kindly tell these friends to leave me. I must pray for the soul of that sinful woman. I must say a personal prayer for her. (*Chume ushers them off. They go reluctantly, chattering excitedly.*) Prayers this evening, as usual. Late afternoon.

CHUME. (*Shouting after.*) Prayers late afternoon as always. Brother Jeroboam says God keep you til then. Are you all right, Brother Jero?

JERO. Who would have thought that she would dare lift her hand against a prophet of God!

CHUME. Women are a plague, brother.

JERO. I had a premonition this morning that women would be my downfall today. But I thought of it only in the spiritual sense.

CHUME. Now you see how it is, Brother Jero.

JERO. From the moment I looked out of my window this morning, I have been tormented one way or another by the daughters of discord.

21

CHUME. (*Eagerly*.) That is how it is with me, brother. Every day. Every morning and night. Only this morning she made me take him to the house of some poor man, whom she says owes her money. She loaded enough on my bicycle to lay a siege for a week, and all the thanks I got was abuse.

JERO. Indeed, it must be a trial, Brother Chume . . . and it requires great. . . . (*He becomes suddenly suspicious.*) Brother Chume, did you say that your wife went to make camp only this morning at the house of a . . . of someone who owes her money?

CHUME. Yes, I took her there myself.

JERO. Er . . . indeed, indeed. (*Coughs.*) Is . . . your wife a trader?

CHUME. Yes, petty trading, you know. Wool, silk, cloth and all that stuff.

JERO. Indeed. Quite an enterprising woman. (*Hems.*) Er . . . where was the house of this man . . . I mean, this man who owes her money?

CHUME. Not very far from here. Ajete settlement, a mile or so from here. I did not even know the place existed until today.

JERO. (*To himself.*) So that is your wife. . . .

CHUME. Did you speak, prophet?

JERO. No, no. I was only thinking how little women have changed since Eve, since Delilah, since Jezebel. But we must be strong of heart. I have my own cross too, Brother Chume. This morning alone I have been thrice in conflict with the daughters of discord. First there was . . . no, never mind that. There is another who crosses my path every day. Goes to swim just over there and then waits for me to be in the midst of my meditation before she swings her hips across here, flaunting her near nakedness before my eyes. . . .

CHUME. (*To himself, with deep feeling.*) I'd willingly change crosses with you.

JERO. What, Brother Chume?

CHUME. I was only praying.

JERO. Ah. That is the only way. But er . . . I wonder really what the will of God would be in this matter. After all, Christ himself was not averse to using the whip when occasion demanded it.

CHUME. (*Eagerly.*) No, he did not hesitate.

JERO. In that case, since, Brother Chume, your wife seems such a wicked, wilful sinner, I think. . . .

22

CHUME. Yes, holy one. . . ?

JERO. You must take her home tonight. . . .

CHUME. Yes. . . .

JERO. And beat her.

CHUME. (*Kneeling, clasps Jero's hand in his.*) Prophet!

JERO. Remember, it must be done in your own house. Never show the discord within your family to the world. Take her home and beat her. (*Chume leaps up and gets his bike.*) And, Brother Chume. . . .

CHUME. Yes, Prophet. . . .

JERO. The Son of God appeared to me again this morning, robed just as he was when he named you my successor. And he placed his burning sword on my shoulder and called me his knight. He gave me a new title . . . but you must tell it to no one—yet.

CHUME. I swear, Brother Jero.

JERO. (*Staring into space.*) He named me the Immaculate Jero, Articulate Hero of Christ's Crusade. (*Pauses, then, with a regal dismissal—*) You may go, Brother Chume.

CHUME. God keep you, Brother Jero—the Immaculate.

JERO. God keep you, brother. (*He sadly fingers the velvet cape.*)

LIGHTS FADE

Scene 4

As Scene 2, i. e. in front of the prophet's home. Later that day. Chume is just wiping off the last crumbs of yams on his plate. Amope watches him.

AMOPE. You can't say I don't try. Hounded out of house by debtors, I still manage to make you a meal.

CHUME. (*Sucking his fingers, sets down his plate.*) It was a good meal, too

AMOPE. I do my share as I've always done. I cooked you your meal. But when I ask you to bring me some clean water, you forget.

CHUME. I did not forget

AMOPE. You keep saying that. Where is it then? Or perhaps the bottles fell off your bicycle on the way and got broken.

CHUME. That's a child's lie, Amope. You are talking to a man.

23

AMOPE. A fine man you are then, when you can't remember a simple thing like a bottle of clean water.

CHUME. I remembered. I just did not bring it. So that is that. And now pack up your things because we're going home. (*Amope stares at him unbelieving.*) Pack up your things; you heard what I said.

AMOPE. (*Scrutinising.*) I thought you were a bit early to get back. You haven't been to work at all. You've been drinking all day.

CHUME. You may think what suits you. You know I never touch any liquor.

AMOPE. You needn't say it as if it was a virtue. You don't drink only because you cannot afford to. That is all the reason there is.

CHUME. Hurry. I have certain work to do when I get home and I don't want you delaying me.

AMOPE. Go then. I am not budging from here till I get my money. (*Chume leaps up, begins to throw her things into the bag. Brother Jero enters, hides and observes them. Amope, quietly:*) I hope you have ropes to tie me on the bicycle, because I don't intend to leave this place unless I am carried out. One pound eight shillings is no child's play. And it is my money not yours. (*Chume has finished packing the bag and is now tying it on to the carrier.*) A messenger's pay isn't that much you know—just in case you've forgotten you're not drawing a Minister's pay. So you better think again if you think I am letting my hardearned money stay in the hands of that good-for-nothing. Just think, only this morning while I sat here, a Sanitary Inspector came along. He looked me all over and he made some notes in his book. Then he said, I suppose, woman, you realise that this place is marked down for slum clearance. This to me, as if I lived here. But you sit down and let your wife be exposed to such insults. And the Sanitary Inspector had a motorcycle too, which is one better than a bicycle.

CHUME. You'd better be ready soon.

AMOPE. A Sanitary Inspector is a better job anyway. You can make something of yourself one way or another. They all do. A little here and a little there, call it bribery if you like, but see where you've got even though you don't drink or smoke or take bribes. He's got a motor-bike . . . anyway, who would want to offer cola to a Chief Messenger?

CHUME. Shut your big mouth!

AMOPE. (*Aghast.*) What did you say?

CHUME. I said shut your big mouth.

AMOPE. To me?

CHUME. Shut your big mouth before I shut it for you. (*Ties the mat round the cross-bar.*) And you'd better start to watch your step from now on. My period of abstinence is over. My cross has been lifted off my shoulders by the prophet.

AMOPE. (*Genuinely distressed.*) He's mad.

CHUME. (*Viciously tying up the mat.*) My period of trial is over. (*Practically strangling the mat.*) If you so much as open your mouth now. . . . (*Gives a further twist to the string.*)

AMOPE. God help me. He's gone mad.

CHUME. (*Imperiously.*) Get on the bike.

AMOPE. (*Backing away.*) I'm not coming with you.

CHUME. I said get on the bike!

AMOPE. Not with you. I'll find my own way home. (*Chume advances on her. Amope screams for help. Brother Jero crosses himself. Chume catches her by the arm but she escapes, runs to the side of the house and beats on the door.*) Help! Open the door for God's sake. Let me in. Let me in. . . . (*Brother Jero grimaces.*) Is anyone in? Let me in for God's sake! Let me in or God will punish you!

JERO. (*Sticking his fingers in his ears.*) Blasphemy!

AMOPE. Prophet! Where's the prophet? (*Chume lifts her bodily.*) Let me down! Police! Police!

CHUME. (*Setting her down.*) If you shout just once more I'll. . . . (*He raises a huge fist. Brother Jero gasps in mock-horror, tut-tuts, covers his eyes with both hands and departs.*)

AMOPE. Ho! You're mad. You're mad.

CHUME. Get on the bike.

AMOPE. Kill me! Kill me!

CHUME. Don't tempt me, woman!

AMOPE. I won't get on that thing unless you kill me first.

CHUME. Woman! (*Two or three neighbours arrive, but keep a respectful distance.*)

AMOPE. Kill me. You'll have to kill me. Everybody come and bear witness. He's going to kill me so come and bear witness. I forgive everyone who has ever done me evil. I forgive all my debtors especially the prophet who has got me into all this trouble. Prophet Jeroboam, I hope you will pray for my soul in heaven. . . .

CHUME. You have no soul, wicked woman.

AMOPE. Brother Jeroboam, curse this man for me. You may keep the velvet cape if you curse this foolish man. I forgive you your debt. Go on, foolish man, kill me. If you don't kill me you won't do well in life.

CHUME. (*Suddenly.*) Shut up!

AMOPE. (*Warming up as more people arrive.*) Bear witness all of you. Tell the prophet I forgive him his debt but he must curse this foolish man to hell. Go on, kill me!

CHUME. (*Who has turned away, forehead knotted in confusion.*) Can't you shut up, woman!

AMOPE. No, you must kill me. . . . (*The crowd hub-bubs all the time, scared as always at the prospect of interfering in man-wife palaver, but throwing in half-hearted tokens of concern—"What's the matter, eh?" "You too keep quiet" "Who are they?" "Where is Brother Jero?" "Do you think we ought to send for the prophet?" "These women are so troublesome! Somebody go and call Brother Jero."*)

CHUME. (*Lifting up Amope's head. She has, in the tradition of the "Kill me" woman, shut her eyes tightly and continued to beat her fists on the prophet's door-step.*) Shut up and listen. Did I hear you say Prophet Jeroboam?

AMOPE. See him now. Let you bear witness. He's going to kill me. . . .

CHUME. I'm not touching you but I will if you don't answer my question.

AMOPE. Kill me . . . kill me. . . .

CHUME. Woman, did you say it was the prophet who owed you money?

AMOPE. Kill me. . . .

CHUME. Is this his house? (*Gives her head a shake.*) Does he live here. . . ?

AMOPE. Kill me . . . kill me. . . .

CHUME. (*Pushing her away in disgust and turning to the crowd. They retreat instinctively.*) Is Brother Jeroboam. . . ?

NEAREST ONE. (*Hastily.*) No, no. I'm not Brother Jero. It's not me.

CHUME. Who said you were? Does the prophet live here?

SAME MAN. Yes. Over there. That house.

CHUME. (*Turns round and stands stock still. Stares at the house for quite some time.)* So . . . so . . . so . . . so. . . . *(The crowd is puzzled over his change of mood. Even Amope looks up wonderingly. Chume walks towards his bicycle, muttering to himself.)* So . . . so . . . suddenly he decides I may beat my wife, eh? For his own convenience. At his own convenience. *(He releases the bundle from the carrier, pushing it down carelessly. He unties the mat also.)*

BYSTANDER. What next is he doing now?

CHUME. *(Mounting his bicycle.)* You stay here and don't move. If I don't find you here when I get back. . . . *(He rides off. They all stare at him in bewilderment.)*

AMOPE. He is quite mad. I have never seen him behave like that.

BYSTANDER. You are sure?

AMOPE. Am I sure? I'm his wife, so I ought to know, shouldn't I?

A WOMAN BYSTANDER. Then you ought to let the prophet see to him. I had a brother once who had the fits and foamed at the mouth every other week. But the prophet cured him. Drove the devils out of him, he did.

AMOPE. This one can't do anything. He's a debtor and that's all he knows. How to dodge his creditors. *(She prepares to unpack her bundle.)*

LIGHTS FADE

Scene 5

The beach. Nightfall.
A man in an elaborate "agbada" outfit, with long train and a cap is standing D. R. *with a sheaf of notes in his hand. He is obviously delivering a speech, but we don't hear it. It is undoubtedly a fire-breathing speech.*
The Prophet Jeroboam stands bolt upright as always, surveying him with lofty compassion.

JERO. I could teach him a trick or two about speech-making. He's a member of the Federal House, a back-bencher but with one eye on a ministerial post. Comes here every day to rehearse his speeches.

27

But he never makes them. Too scared. (*Pause. The prophet continues to study the Member.*) Poor fish. (*Chuckles and looks away.*) Odo, I had almost forgotten Brother Chume. By now he ought to have beaten his wife senseless. Pity! That means I've lost him. He is fulfilled and no longer needs me. True, he still has to become a Chief Clerk. But I have lost him as the one who was most dependent on me. . . . Never mind, it was a good price to pay for getting rid of my creditor. . . . (*Goes back to the Member.*) Now he . . . he is already a member of my flock. He does not know it of course, but he is a follower. All I need do is claim him. Call him and say to him, My dear Member of the House, your place awaits you. . . . Or do you doubt it? Watch me go to work on him. (*Raises his voice.*) My dear brother in Jesus! (*The Member stops, looks around, resumes his speech.*) Dear brother, do I not know you? (*Member stops, looks round again.*) Yes, you. In God's name, do I know You? (*Member approaches slowly.*) Yes indeed. It is you. And you come as it was predicted. Do you not perhaps remember me? (*Member looks at him scornfully.*) Then you cannot be of the Lord. In another world, in another body, we met, and my message was for you. . . . (*The Member turns his back impatiently.*)

MEMBER. (*With great pomposity.*) Go and practice your fraudulences on another person of greater gullibility.

JERO. (*Very kindly, smiling.*) Indeed the matter is quite plain. You are not of the Lord. And yet such is the mystery of God's ways that his favour has lighted upon you . . . Minister . . . Minister by the grace of God . . . (*The Member stops dead.*) Yes, brother, we have met. I saw this country plunged into strife. I saw the mustering of men, gathered in the name of peace through strength. And at a desk, in a large gilt room, great men of the land awaited your decision. Emissaries of foreign nations hung on your word, and on the door leading into your office, I read the words, Minister for War . . . (*The Member turns round slowly.*) . . . It is a position of power. But are you of the Lord? Are you in fact worthy? Must I, when I have looked into your soul, as the Lord has commanded me to do, must I pray to the Lord to remove this mantle from your shoulders and place it on a more God-fearing man? (*The Member moves forward unconsciously. The prophet gestures him to stay where he is. Slowly—*) Yes . . . I think I see Satan in your eyes. I see him entrenched in your eyes . . . (*The

28

Member grows fearful, raises his arms in half-supplication . . .)
The Minister for War would be the most powerful position in the
land. The Lord knows best, but he has empowered his lieutenants
on earth to intercede where necessary. We can reach him by fasting
and by prayer . . . we can make recommendations . . . brother,
are you of God or are you ranged among his enemies. . . ? *(Jeroboam's voice fades away and the light also dims on him as another
voice—Chume's—is heard long before he is seen. Chume enters
from* D. L., *agitated and talking to himself.)*
CHUME. . . . What for . . . why, why, why, why 'e do 'am?
For two years 'e no let me beat that woman. Why? No because
God no like 'am. That one no fool me any more. 'E no be man of
God. 'E say 'in sleep for beach whether 'e rain or cold but that
one too na big lie. The man get house and 'e sleep there every night.
But 'im get peace for 'in house, why 'e no let me get peace for
mine? Wetin I do for 'am? Anyway, how they come meet? Where?
When? What time 'e know say na my wife? Why 'e dey protect
'am from me? Perhaps na my woman dey give 'am chop and in return he promise to see say 'in husband no beat 'am. A . . . ah,
give 'am clothes, give 'am food and all comforts and necessities, and
for exchange, 'in go see that 'in husband no beat 'am. . . .
Mmmmmm. *(He shakes his head.)* No, is not possible. I no believe
that. If na so, how they come quarrel then. Why she go sit for
front of 'in house demand all money. I no beat 'am yet. . . . *(He
stops suddenly. His eyes slowly distend.)* Almighty! Chume, fool!
O God, my life done spoil. My life done spoil finish. O God a no'
get eyes for my head. Na lie. Na big lie. Na pretence 'e de pretend
that wicked womạn! She no go collect nutin! She no' mean to sleep
for outside house. The prophet na 'in lover. As soon as 'e dark, she
go in to met 'in man. O God, wetin a do for you wey you go
spoil my life so? Wetin make you vex for me so? I offend you?
Chume, foolish man, your life done spoil. Your life don spoil yeah,
ye . . . ah ah, ye . . . ah, they done ruin Chume for life . . .
ye . . . ah, ye . . . ah, ... *(He goes off, his cries dying offstage. Lights up slowly on Jero. The Member is seen kneeling now
at Brother Jero's feet, hands clasped and shut eyes raised to
heaven. . . .)*
JERO. *(His voice gaining volume.)* Protect him therefore. Protect
him when he must lead this country as his great ancestors have

done. He comes from the great warriors of the land. In his innocence he was not aware of this heritage. But you know everything and you plan it all. There is no end, no beginning. . . . (*Chume rushes in, brandishing a cutlass.*)

CHUME. Adulterer! Woman-thief! Na today a go finish you! (*Jero looks round.*)

JERO. God save us! (*Flees.*)

MEMBER. (*Unaware of what is happening.*) Amen. (*Chume follows out Jero, murder-bent.*) Amen. Amen. (*Opens his eyes.*) Thank you, proph . . . (*He looks right, left, back, front, but he finds the prophet has really disappeared.*) Prophet! Prophet! (*Turns sharply and rapidly in every direction, shouting.*) Prophet, where are you? Where have you gone? Prohet! Don't leave me, prophet, don't leave me! (*He looks up slowly, with awe.*) Vanished. Transported. Utterly transmuted. I knew it. I knew I stood in the presence of God. . . . (*He bows his head, standing. Jero enters quite collected, and points to the convert.*)

JERO. You heard him. With your own ears you heard him. By to-morrow, the whole town have heard about the miraculous disappearance of Brother Jeroboam. Testified to and witnessed by no less a person than one of the elected rulers of the country. . . .

MEMBER. (*Goes to sit on the mound.*) I must await his return. If I show faith, he will show himself again to me. . . . (*Leaps up as he is about to sit.*) This is holy ground. (*Takes off his shoes and sits. Gets up again.*) I must hear further from him. Perhaps he has gone to learn more about this ministerial post. . . . (*Sits.*)

JERO. I have already sent for the police. It is a pity about Chume. But he has given me a fright, and no prophet likes to be frightened. With the influence of that nincompoop I should succeed in getting him certified with ease. A year in the lunatic asylum would do him good anyway. (*The Member is already nodding.*) Good . . . he is falling asleep. When I appear again to him he'll think I have just fallen from the sky. Then I'll tell him that Satan just sent one of his emissaries into the world under the name of Chume, and that he had better put him in a straitjacket at once. . . . And so the day is saved. The police will call on me here as soon as they catch Chume. And it looks as if it is not quite time for the fulfillment of that spiteful man's prophecy. (*He picks up a pebble and throws it at the Member. At the same time a ring of red or some equally*

30

startling colour plays on his head forming a sort of halo. The peni-
tent wakes with a start, stares, open-mouthed, and falls flat on his
face, whispering in rapt awe—)
PENITENT. "Master!"

BLACKOUT

THE END

PROPERTY PLOT

SCENE 1

Personal:

Canvas pouch ⎱
Divine rod   ⎰ (Jero)

SCENE 2

Off Stage, L.:

Bicycle, with bell and carrier basket
Stool and mat, on bicycle
Bag, in carrier basket, containing:
    Pie plates (2)
    Corked bottles of water (2)
    Small saucepans (2)
    Knife, fork and spoon
    Brown paper packages, taped shut (2)
    Brown paper package, tied with string
    Yam
    Small brazier, covered with paper
    Ovaltine jar
    Can with brown paper top
    Box of matches
Calabash bowl, with cover ⎫
Fish, in bowl   ⎬ (Trader Woman)
Fan   ⎭
2 drums and sticks (Drummer boy)
Small notebook ⎫
Pencil   ⎬ (Amope)
Cola nut (to chew) ⎭

SCENE 3

On Stage:

Palm.tree
Heap of sand, with assorted empty bottles in it
Small mirror, in sand
Rosary and cross, hanging from bottle

Off Stage L.:

Bloodstained stick (Woman)
Tambourines (Congregation)

Personal:

Gold watch (Jero)

32

On Stage:
  Amope's bag and gear (as in Scene 2)

SCENE 5

On Stage:
  Pebbles

Off Stage, L.:
  Cutlass (Chume)

Personal:
  Papers for speech (Member of Parliament)

COSTUME PLOT

White velvet robe (Jero)
White cotton vestment with red cross (Jero)
1 red and yellow check sock, and 1 solid red sock (Jero)
Brown print head wrap with under cloth of purple print (Amope)
Pink striped top (Amope)
Blue and red print waist tie (Amope)
Blue and red print skirt (Amope)
Beige top (Trader Woman)
Blue, orange, red "square print" skirt (Trader Woman)
2 pc. maroon and brown striped buba and pants (Drummer)
Blue vestment (Old Tutor)
Blue upholstery-like fabric agbada and pants (Member of Parliament)
2 pc. khaki uniform (jacket and shorts) (Chume)

The Strong Breed

A Play by Wole Soyinka

CAST OF CHARACTERS

EMAN, *a stranger*

SUNMA, *Jaguna's daughter*

IFADA, *an idiot*

A GIRL

JAGUNA

OROGE

ATTENDANT STALWARTS, *the villagers*

From Eman's past—

OLD MAN, *his father*

OMAE, *his betrothed*

TUTOR

PRIEST

ATTENDANTS, *the villagers*

The scenes are described briefly, but very often a darkened stage with lit areas will not only suffice but is necessary. Except for the one indicated place, there can be no break in the action. A distracting scene-change would be ruinous.

The Strong Breed

*A mud house, with space in front of it. Eman, in light
buba and trousers stands at the window, looking out. Inside, Sunma is clearing the table of what looks like a
modest clinic, putting the things away in a cupboard.
Another rough table in the room is piled with exercise
books, two or three worn text-books, etc. Sunma appears
agitated. Outside, just below the window crouches Ifada.
He looks up with a shy smile from time to time, waiting
for Eman to notice him.*

SUNMA. (*Hesitant.*) You will have to make up your mind soon
Eman. The lorry leaves very shortly. (*As Eman does not answer,
Sunma continues her work, more nervously. Two villagers, obvious
travellers, pass hurriedly in front of the house, the man has a small
raffia sack, the woman a cloth-covered basket, the man enters first,
turns and urges the woman who is just emerging to hurry. When
Sunma sees them, her tone is more intense.*) Eman, are we going or
aren't we? You will leave it till too late.
EMAN. (*Quietly.*) There is still time—if you want to go.
SUNMA. If I want to go . . . and you? (*Eman makes no reply.
Sunma, bitterly:*) You don't really want to leave here. You never
want to go away—even for a minute. (*Ifada continues his antics.
Eman eventually pats him on the head and the boy grins happily.
Leaps up suddenly and returns with a basket of oranges which he
offers to Eman.*)
EMAN. Something for today's festival enh? (*Ifada nods, grin-
ning.*) They look ripe—that's a change.
SUNMA. (*She has gone inside the room, looks round the door.*)
Did you call me?
EMAN. No. (*She goes back.*) And what will you do tonight Ifada?
Will you take part in the dancing? Or perhaps you will mount
your own masquerade? (*Ifada shakes his head, regretfully.*) You
won't? So you haven't any? But you would like to own one. (*Ifada
nods eagerly.*) Then why don't you make your own? (*Ifada stares,*

37

puzzled by this idea.) Sunma will let you have some cloth you know. And bits of wool . . .

SUNMA. (*Coming out.*) Who are you talking to Eman?

EMAN. Ifada. I am trying to persuade him to join the young maskers.

SUNMA. (*Losing control.*) What does he want here? Why is he hanging round us?

EMAN. (*Amazed.*) What . . . ? I said Ifada. Ifada.

SUNMA. Just tell him to go away. Let him go and play somewhere else!

EMAN. What is this? Hasn't he always played here?

SUNMA. I don't want him here. (*Rushes to the window.*) Get away idiot. Don't bring your foolish face here any more, do you hear? Go on, go away from here . . .

EMAN. (*Restraining her.*) Control yourself Sunma. What on earth has got into you? (*Ifada, hurt and bewildered, backs slowly away.*)

SUNMA. He comes crawling round here like some horrible insect. I never want to lay my eyes on him again.

EMAN. I don't understand. It *is* Ifada you know. Ifada! The unfortunate one who runs errands for you and doesn't hurt a soul.

SUNMA. I cannot bear the sight of him.

EMAN. You can't do what? It can't be two days since he last fetched water for you.

SUNMA. What else can he do except that? He is useless. Just because we have been kind to him. . . . Others would have put him in an asylum.

EMAN. You are not making sense. He is not a madman, he is just a little more unlucky than other children. (*Looks keenly at her.*) But what is the matter?

SUNMA. It is nothing. I only wish we had sent him off to one of those places for creatures like him.

EMAN. He is quite happy here. He doesn't bother anyone and he makes himself useful.

SUNMA. Useful! Is that one of any use to anybody? Boys of his age are already earning a living but all he can do is hang around and drool at the mouth.

EMAN. But he does work. You know he does a lot for you.

SUNMA. Does he? And what about the farm you started for him! Does he ever work on it? Or have you forgotten that it was really for Ifada you cleared that bush. Now you have to go and work it yourself. You spend all your time on it and you have no room for anything else.

EMAN. That wasn't his fault. I should first have asked him if he was fond of farming.

SUNMA. Oh, so he càn choose? As if he should not be thankful for being allowed to live.

EMAN. Sunma!

SUNMA. He does not like farming but he knows how to feast on it as soon . . .

EMAN. But I want him to. I encourage him.

SUNMA. Well keep him. I don't want to see him any more.

EMAN. (*After some moments.*) But why? You cannot be telling all the truth. What has he done?

SUNMA. The sight of him fills me with revulsion.

EMAN. (*Goes to her and holds her.*) What really is it? (*Sunma avoids his eyes.*) It is almost as if you are forcing yourself to hate him. Why?

SUNMA. That is not true. Why should I?

EMAN. Then what is the secret? You've even played with him before.

SUNMA. I have always merely tolerated him. But I cannot anymore. Suddenly my disgust won't take him any more. Perhaps . . . perhaps it is the new year. Yes, yes, it must be the new year.

EMAN. I don't believe that.

SUNMA. It must be. I am a woman, and these things matter. I don't want a mis-shape near me. Surely for one day in the year, I may demand some wholesomeness.

EMAN. I do not understand you. (*Sunma is silent.*) It was cruel of you. And to Ifada who is so helpless and alone. We are the only friends he has.

SUNMA. No, just you. I have told you, with me it has always been only an act of kindness. And now I haven't any pity left for him.

EMAN. No. He is not a wholesome being. (*He turns back to looking through the window.*)

SUNMA. (*Half pleading.*) Ifada can rouse your pity. And yet if anything, I need more kindness from you. Every time my weakness betrays me, you close your mind against me . . . Eman . . . Eman . . . (*A girl comes in view, dragging an effigy by a rope attached to one of its legs. She stands for a while gazing at Eman. Ifada, who has crept back shyly to his accustomed position, be-*

comes somewhat excited when he sees the effigy. The girl is un-smiling. She possesses in fact, a kind of inscrutability which does not make her hard but is unsettling.)

GIRL. Is the teacher in?

EMAN. (*Smiling.*) No.

GIRL. Where is he gone?

EMAN. I don't really know. Shall I ask?

GIRL. Yes, do.

EMAN. (*Turning slightly.*) Sunma, a girl outside wants to know . . . (*Sunma turns away, goes into the inside room.*) Oh. (*Returns to the girl, but his slight gaiety is lost.*) There is no one at home who can tell me.

GIRL. Why are you not in?

EMAN. I don't really know. Maybe I went somewhere.

GIRL. All right. I will wait until you get back. (*She pulls the effigy to her, sits down.*)

EMAN. (*Slowly regaining his amusement.*) So you are all ready for the new year.

GIRL. (*Without turning round.*) I am not going to the festival.

EMAN. Then why have you got that?

GIRL. Do you mean my carrier? I am unwell you know. My mother says it will take away my sickness with the old year.

EMAN. Won't you share the carrier with your playmates?

GIRL. Oh, no. Don't you know I play alone? The other children won't come near me. Their mothers would beat them.

EMAN. But I have never seen you here. Why don't you come to the clinic?

GIRL. My mother said no. (*Gets up, begins to move off.*)

EMAN. You are not going away?

GIRL. I must not stay talking to you. If my mother caught me . . .

EMAN. All right, tell me what you want before you go.

GIRL. (*Stops. For some moments she remains silent.*) I must have some clothes for my carrier.

EMAN. Is that all? You wait a moment. (*Sunma comes out as he takes down a buba from the wall. She goes to the window and glares almost with hatred at the girl. The girl retreats hastily, still impassive.*) By the way Sunma, do you know who that girl is?

SUNMA. I hope you don't really mean to give her that.

EMAN. Why not? I hardly ever use it.

SUNMA. Just the same don't give it to her. She is not a child. She is as evil as the rest of them.

EMAN. What has got into you today?

SUNMA. All right, all right. Do what you wish. (*She withdraws. Baffled, Eman returns to the window.*)

EMAN. Here . . . will this do? Come and look at it.

GIRL. Throw it.

EMAN. What is the matter? I am not going to eat you.

GIRL. No one lets me come near them.

EMAN. But I am not afraid of catching your disease.

GIRL. Throw it. (*Eman shrugs and tosses the buba. She takes it without a word and slips it on the effigy, completely absorbed in the task. Eman watches for a while, then joins Sunma in the inner room. Girl, after a long, cool survey of Ifada.*) There is no one else. Would you like to play? (*Ifada nods eagerly, quite excited.*) You will have to get a stick. (*Ifada rushes around, finds a big stick and whirls it aloft, bearing down on the carrier.*) Wait. I don't want you to spoil it. If it gets torn I shall drive you away. Now, let me see how you are going to beat it. (*Ifada hits it gently.*) You may hit harder than that. As long as there is something left to hang at the end. (*She appraises him up and down.*) You are not very tall. . . . Will you be able to hang it from a tree? (*Ifada nods, grinning happily.*) You will hang it up and I will set fire to it. (*Then with surprising venom.*) But just because you are helping me, don't think it is going to cure you. I am the one who will get well by tomorrow, do you understand? It is my carrier and it is for me alone. (*She pulls at the rope to make sure that it is well attached to the leg.*) Let us go. (*She begins to walk off, dragging the effigy in the dust. Ifada remains where he is for some moments, seemingly puzzled. Then his face breaks into a large grin and he leaps after the procession, belabouring the effigy with all his strength. The stage remains empty for some moments. Then the horn of a lorry is sounded and Sunma rushes out. The hooting continues for some time with a rhythmic pattern. Eman comes out.*)

EMAN. I am going to the village . . . I shan't be back before nightfall.

SUNMA. (*Blankly.*) Yes.

EMAN. (*Hesitates.*) Well what do you want me to do?

SUNMA. The lorry was hooting just now.

41

EMAN. I didn't hear it.

SUNMA. It will leave in a few minutes. And you did promise we could go away.

EMAN. I promised nothing. Will you go home by yourself or shall I come back for you?

SUNMA. You don't even want me here?

EMAN. But you do have to go home haven't you?

SUNMA. I had hoped we would watch the new year together—in some other place.

EMAN. Why do you continue to say what distresses you?

SUNMA. Because you will not listen to me. Why do you continue to stay where nobody wants you?

EMAN. That is not true.

SUNMA. It is. You are wasting your life on people who really want you out of their way.

EMAN. You don't know what you are saying.

SUNMA. You think they love you? Do you think they care at all for what you—or I—do for them?

EMAN. *Them?* These are your own people. Sometimes you talk as if you were a stranger too.

SUNMA. I wonder if I really sprang from here. I know they are evil and I am not. From the oldest to the smallest child, they are nourished in evil and unwholesomeness in which I have no part.

EMAN. You knew this when you returned?

SUNMA. You reproach me then for trying at all?

EMAN. I reproach you with nothing. But you must leave me out of your plans. I can have no part in them.

SUNMA. (*Nearly pleading.*) Once I could have run away. I would have gone and never looked back.

EMAN. I cannot listen when you talk like that.

SUNMA. I swear to you, I do not mind what happens afterwards. But you must help me tear myself away from here. I can no longer do it by myself. . . . It is only a little thing. And we have worked so hard this past year . . . surely we can go away for a week . . . even a few days would be enough.

EMAN. I have told you Sunma. . . .

SUNMA. (*Desperately.*) Two days Eman. Only two days.

EMAN. (*Distressed.*) But I tell you I have no wish to go.

SUNMA. (*Suddenly angry.*) Are you so afraid then?

EMAN. Me? Afraid of what?

42

SUNMA. You think you will not want to come back.

EMAN. (*Pitying.*) You cannot hurt me that way.

SUNMA. Then why won't you leave here, even for an hour? If you are so sure that your life is settled here, why are you afraid to do this thing for me? What is so wrong that you will not go into the next town for a day or two?

EMAN. I do not want to. I don't have to persuade you, or myself about anything. I simply have no desire to go away.

SUNMA. (*This quiet confidence appears to incense her.*) You are afraid. You accuse me of losing my sense of mission, but you are afraid to put yours to the test.

EMAN. You are wrong Sunma. I have no sense of mission. But I have found peace here and I am content with that.

SUNMA. I have not. For a while I thought that too, but I found there could be no peace in the midst of so much cruelty. Eman, tonight at least, the last night of the old year . . .

EMAN. No Sunma. I find this too distressing; you should go home now.

SUNMA. It is the time for making changes in one's life Eman. Let us breathe in the new year away from here.

EMAN. You are hurting yourself.

SUNMA. Tonight. Only tonight. We will come back tomorrow, as early as you like. But let us go away for this one night. Don't let another year break on me in this place . . . you don't know how important it is to me, but I will tell you, I will tell you on the way . . . but we must not be here today, Eman, do this one thing for me.

EMAN. (*Sadly.*) I cannot.

SUNMA. (*Suddenly calm.*) I was a fool to think it would be otherwise. The whole village may use you as they will but for me there is nothing. Sometimes I think you believe that doing anything for me makes you unfaithful to some part of your life. If it was a woman then I pity her for what she must have suffered. (*Eman winces and hardens slowly. Sunma notices nothing.*) Keeping faith with so much is slowly making you inhuman. (*Seeing the change in Eman.*) Eman. Eman. What is it? (*As she goes towards him, Eman goes into the house. Sunma, apprehensive, follows him.*) What did I say? Eman, forgive me, forgive me please. (*Eman remains facing into the slow darkness of the room. Sunma, distressed, cannot decide what to do.*) I swear I did not know . . . I would not have said it for all the world. (*A lorry is heard taking off somewhere nearby. The sound comes up and slowly fades away into the distance. Sunma starts visibly, goes slowly to the window. As the sound dies off, to herself.*) What happens now?

EMAN. (*Joining her at the window.*) What did you say?

SUNMA. Nothing.

EMAN. Was that not the lorry going off?

SUNMA. It was.

EMAN. I am sorry I could not help you.

SUNMA. (*About to speak, changes her mind.*)

EMAN. I think you ought to go home now.

SUNMA. No, don't send me away. It is the least you can do for me. Let me stay here until all the noise is over.

EMAN. But are you not needed at home? You have a part in the festival.

SUNMA. I have renounced it; I am Jaguna's eldest daughter only in name.

EMAN. Renouncing one's self is not so easy—surely you know that.

SUNMA. I do not want to talk about it. Will you at least let us be together tonight?

EMAN. But . . .

SUNMA. Unless you are afraid my father will accuse you of harbouring me.

EMAN. All right, we will go out together.

SUNMA. Go out? I want us to stay here.

EMAN. When there is so much going on outside?

SUNMA. Some day you will wish that you went away when I tried to make you.

EMAN. Are we going back to that?

SUNMA. No. I promise you I will not recall it again. But you must know that it was also for your sake that I tried to get us away.

EMAN. For me? How?

SUNMA. By yourself you can do nothing here. Have you not noticed how tightly we shut out strangers? Even if you lived here for a lifetime, you would remain a stranger.

EMAN. Perhaps that is what I like. There is peace in being a stranger.

SUNMA. For a while perhaps. But they would reject you in the end. I tell you it is only I who stand between you and contempt.

44

And because of this you have earned their hatred. I don't know why I say this now, except that somehow, I feel that it no longer matters. It is only I who have stood between you and much humiliation.

EMAN. Think carefully before you say any more. I am incapable of feeling indebted to you. This will make no difference at all.

SUNMA. I ask for nothing. But you must know it all the same. It is true I had not the strength to go by myself. And I must confess this now, if you had come with me, I would have done everything to keep you from returning.

EMAN. I know that.

SUNMA. You see, I bare myself to you. For days I had thought it over, this was to be a new beginning for us. And I placed my fate wholly in your hands. Now the thought will not leave me, I have a feeling which will not be shaken off, that in some way, you have tonight totally destroyed my life.

EMAN. You are depressed, you don't know what you are saying.

SUNMA. Don't think I am accusing you. I say all this only because I cannot help it.

EMAN. We must not remain shut up here. Let us go and be part of the living.

SUNMA. No. Leave them alone.

EMAN. Surely you don't want to stay indoors when the whole town is alive with rejoicing.

SUNMA. Rejoicing! Is that what it seems to you? No, let us remain here. Whatever happens I must not go out until all this is over. (*There is a silence. It has grown much darker.*)

EMAN. I shall light the lamp.

SUNMA. (*Eager to do something.*) No, let me do it. (*She goes into the inner room. Eman paces the room, stops by a shelf and toys with the seeds in an "ayo" board, takes down the whole board and places it on a table, playing by himself. The girl is now seen coming back, still dragging her "carrier." Ifada brings up the rear as before. As he comes round the corner of the house two men emerge from the shadows. A sack is thrown over Ifada's head, the rope is pulled tight rendering him instantly helpless. The girl has reached the front of the house before she turns round at the sound of scuffle. She is in time to see Ifada thrown over the shoulders and borne away. Her face betraying no emotion at all, the girl backs slowly away, turns and flees, leaving the "carrier" behind.*)

45

Sunma enters, carrying two kerosene lamps. She hangs one up from the wall.)

EMAN. One is enough.

SUNMA. I want to leave one outside. (*She goes out, hangs the lamp from a nail just above the door. As she turns she sees the effigy and gasps. Eman rushes out.*)

EMAN. What is it? Oh, is that what frightened you?

SUNMA. I thought . . . I didn't really see it properly. (*Eman goes towards the object, stoops to pick it up.*)

EMAN. It must belong to that sick girl.

SUNMA. Don't touch it.

EMAN. Let's keep it for her.

SUNMA. Leave it alone. Don't touch it, Eman.

EMAN. (*Shrugs and goes back.*) You are very nervous.

SUNMA. Let us go in.

EMAN. Wait. (*He detains her by the door, under the lamp.*) I know there is something more than you've told me. What are you afraid of tonight?

SUNMA. I was only scared by that thing. There is nothing else.

EMAN. I am not blind Sunma. It is true I would not run away when you wanted me to, but that does not mean I do not feel things. What does tonight really mean that it makes you so helpless?

SUNMA. It is only a mood. And your indifference to me . . . let us go in. (*Eman moves aside and she enters; he remains there for a moment and then follows. She fiddles with the lamp, looks vaguely round the room, then goes and shuts the door, bolting it. When she turns, it is to meet Eman's eyes, questioning.*) There is a cold wind coming in. (*Eman keeps his gaze on her.*) It was getting cold. (*She moves guiltily to the table and stands by the "ayo" board, rearranging the seeds. Eman remains where he is a few moments, then brings a stool and sits opposite her. She sits down also and they begin to play in silence.*) It is a year now since you came here, but no one knows who you really are or what brought you. We never really talked, you and I. (*There is another silence.*) I am not trying to share your life. I know you too well by now. But at least we have worked together since you came. Is there nothing at all I deserve to know?

EMAN. Let me continue a stranger—especially to you. Those who

46

have much to give fulfil themselves only when they do so in total loneliness.

SUNMA. Then there is no love in what you do.

EMAN. There is. Love comes to me more easily with strangers.

SUNMA. That is unnatural.

EMAN. I do not find that. I know that I find consummation only when I have spent myself for a total stranger.   .

SUNMA. It seems unnatural to me. But then I am a woman. I have a woman's longings and weaknesses. And the ties of blood are very strong in me.

EMAN. (*Smiling.*) You think I have cut loose from all these—ties of blood.

SUNMA. Sometimes you are so inhuman.

EMAN. I don't know what that means. But I am very much my father's son. (*They play in silence. Suddenly Eman pauses listening.*) Did you hear that?

SUNMA. (*Quickly.*) I heard nothing. . . . It's your turn.

EMAN. Perhaps some of the mummers are coming this way. (*Eman about to play, leaps up suddenly.*)

SUNMA. What is it? Don't you want to play anymore? (*Eman moves to the door.*) No. Don't go out Eman.

EMAN. If it's the dancers I want to ask them to stay. At least we won't have to miss everything.

SUNMA. No, No, Don't open the door. Let us keep out everyone tonight. (*A terrified and disordered figure bursts suddenly round the corner, past the window and begins hammering at the door. It is Ifada. Desperate with terror, he pounds madly at the door, dumb-moaning all the while.*)

EMAN. Isn't that Ifada?

SUNMA. They are only fooling about. Don't pay any attention.

EMAN. (*Looks round the window.*) That is Ifada. (*Begins to unbolt the door.*)

SUNMA. (*Pulling at his hands.*) It is only a trick they are playing on you. Don't take any notice Eman.

EMAN. What are you saying? The boy is out of his senses with fear.

SUNMA. No, No. Don't interfere Eman. For God's sake don't interfere.

EMAN. Do you know something of this then?

47

SUNMA. You are a stranger here Eman. Just leave us alone and go your own way. There is nothing you can do.

EMAN. (*He tries to push her out of the way but she clings fiercely to him.*) Have you gone mad? I tell you the boy must come in.

SUNMA. Why won't you listen to me, Eman? I tell you it's none of your business. For your own sake do as I say. (*Eman pushes her off, unbolts the door. Ifada rushes in, clasps Eman round the knees, dumb-moaning against his legs.*)

EMAN. (*Manages to re-bolt the door.*) What is it Ifada? What is the matter? (*Shouts and voices are heard coming nearer the house.*)

SUNMA. Before it is too late, let him go. For once Eman, believe what I tell you. Don't harbour him or you will regret it all your life. (*Eman tries to calm Ifada who becomes more and more abject as the outside voices get nearer.*)

EMAN. What have they done to him? At least tell me that. What is going on Sunma?

SUNMA. (*With sudden venom.*) Monster! Could you not take your self somewhere else?

EMAN. Stop talking like that.

SUNMA. He could have run into the bush couldn't he? Toad! Why must he follow us with his own disasters!

VOICES OUTSIDE. It's here . . . round the back . . . spread, spread . . . this way . . . no, head him off . . . use the bush path and head him off . . . get some more lights . . . (*Eman listens. Lifts Ifada bodily and carries him into the inner room. Returns at once, shutting the door behind him.*)

SUNMA. (*Slumps into a chair, resigned.*) You always follow your own way.

JAGUNA. (*Comes round the corner followed by Oroge and three men, one bearing a torch.*) I knew he would come here.

OROGE. I hope our friend won't make trouble.

JAGUNA. He had better not. You, recall all the men and tell them to surround the house.

OROGE. But he may not be in the house after all.

JAGUNA. I know he is here . . . (*To the men.*) . . . go on, do as I say. (*He bangs on the door.*) Teacher, open your door. . . . You two stay by the door. If I need you I will call you. (*Eman opens the door. Jaguna speaks as he enters.*) We know he is here.

EMAN. Who?

JAGUNA. Don't let us waste time. We are grown men, teacher. You understand me and I understand you. But we must take back the boy.

EMAN. This is my house.

JAGUNA. Daughter, you'd better tell your friend. I don't think he quite knows our ways. Tell him why he must give up the boy.

SUNMA. Father, I . . .

JAGUNA. Are you going to tell him or aren't you?

SUNMA. Father, I beg you, leave us alone tonight . . .

JAGUNA. I thought you might be a hindrance. Go home then if you will not use your sense.

SUNMA. But there are other ways . . .

JAGUNA. (*Turning to the men.*) See that she gets home. I no longer trust her. If she gives trouble carry her. And see that the women stay with her until all this is over. (*Sunma departs, accompanied by one of the men.*) Now, teacher . . .

OROGE. (*Restrains him.*) You see Mister Eman, it is like this. Right now, nobody knows that Ifada has taken refuge here. No one except us and our men—and they know how to keep their mouths shut. We don't want to have to burn down the house, you see, but if the word gets around, we would have no choice.

JAGUNA. In fact, it may be too late already. A carrier should end up in the bush, not in a house. Anyone who doesn't guard his door when the carrier goes by has himself to blame. A contaminated house should be burnt down.

OROGE. But we are willing to let it pass. Only, you must bring him out quickly.

EMAN. Alright. But at least you will let me ask you something.

JAGUNA. What is there to ask? Don't you understand what we have told you?

EMAN. Yes. But why did you pick on a helpless boy? Obviously he is not willing. In my home, we believe that a man should be willing.

OROGE. Mister Eman, I don't think you quite understand. This is not a simple matter at all. I don't know what you do, but here, it is not a cheap task for anybody. No one in his senses would do such a job. Why do you think we give refuge to idiots like him? We don't know where he came from. One morning, he is simply there, just like that. From nowhere at all. You see, there is a purpose in that.

JAGUNA. We only waste time.

OROGE. Jaguna, be patient. After all, the man has been with us for some time now and deserves to know. The evil of the old year is no light thing to load on any man's head.

EMAN. I know something about that.

OROGE. You do? (*Turns to Jaguna who snorts impatiently.*) You see, I told you so didn't I? From the moment you came I saw you were one of the knowing ones.

JAGUNA. Then let him behave like a man and give back the boy.

EMAN. It is you who are not behaving like men.

JAGUNA. (*Advances aggressively.*) That is a quick mouth you have . . .

OROGE. Patience Jaguna. . . . If you want the new year to be soft there must be no deeds of anger. What did you mean, my friend?

EMAN. It is a simple thing. A village which cannot produce its own carrier contains no men.

JAGUNA. Enough. Let there be no more talk or this business will be ruined by some rashness. You . . . come inside. Bring the boy out, he must be in the room there.

EMAN. Wait. (*The men hesitate.*)

JAGUNA. (*Hitting the nearer one and propelling him forward.*) Go on. Have you changed masters now that you listen to what he says?

OROGE. (*Sadly.*) I am sorry you would not understand Mister Eman. But you ought to know that no carrier may return to the village. If he does, the people will stone him to death. It has happened before. Surely it is too much to ask a man to give up his own soil.

EMAN. I know others who have done more. (*Ifada is brought out, abjectly dumb-moaning.*) You can see him with your own eyes. Does it really have meaning to use one as unwilling as that.

OROGE. (*Smiling.*) He shall be willing. Not only willing but actually joyous. I am the one who prepares them all, and I have seen worse. This one escaped before I began to prepare him for the event. But you will see him later tonight, the most joyous creature in the festival. Then perhaps you will understand.

EMAN. Then it is only a deceit. Do you believe the spirit of a new year is so easily fooled?

JAGUNA. Take him out. (*The men carry out Ifada.*) You see, it is so easy to talk. You say there are no men in this village because they cannot provide a willing carrier. And yet I heard Oroge tell you we only use strangers. There is only one other stranger in the village, but I have not heard him offer himself. (*Spits.*) It is so easy to talk is it not? (*He turns his back on him. They go off, taking Ifada with them, limp and silent. The only sign of life is that he strains his neck to keep his eyes on Eman till the very moment that he disappears from sight. Eman is standing where they left him, staring after the group. A black-out lasting no more than a minute. The lights come up slowly and Ifada is seen returning to the house. He stops at the window and looks in. Seeing no one, he bangs on the sill. Appears surprised that there is no response. He slithers down on his favourite spot, then sees the effigy still lying where the girl had dropped it in her flight. After some hesitation, he goes towards it, begins to strip it of the clothing. Just then the girl comes in.*)

GIRL. Hey, leave that alone. You know it is mine. (*Ifada pauses, then speeds up his action.*) I said it is mine. Leave it where you found it. (*She rushes at him and begins to struggle for possession of the carrier.*) Thief! Thief! Let it go, it is mine. Let it go. You animal, just because I let you play with it. Idiot! Idiot! (*The struggle becomes quite violent. The girl is hanging to the effigy and Ifada lifts her with it, flinging her all about. The girl hangs on grimly.*) You are spoiling it . . . why don't you get your own? Thief!? Let it go you thief! (*Sunma comes in walking very fast, throwing apprehensive glances over her shoulder. Seeing the two children, she becomes immediately angry. Advances on them.*)

SUNMA. So you've made this place your playground. Get away you untrained pigs. Get out of here. (*Ifada flees at once, the girl retreats also, retaining possession of the "carrier." Sunma goes to the door. She has her hand on the door when the significance of Ifada's presence strikes her for the first time. She stands rooted to the spot, then turns slowly round.*) Ifada! What are you doing here? (*Ifada is bewildered. Sunma turns suddenly and rushes into the house, flying into the inner room and out again.*) Eman! Eman! Eman! (*She rushes outside.*) Where did he go? Where did they take him? (*Ifada distressed, points. Sunma seizes him by the arm,*)

51

drags him off.) Take me there at once. God help you if we are too late. You loathsome thing, if you have let him suffer . . . (*Her voice fades into other shouts, running footsteps, banged tins, bells, dogs, etc., rising in volume. It is a narrow passage-way between two mud-houses. At the far end one man after another is seen running across the entry, the noise dying off gradually. About half-way down the passage, Eman is crouching against the wall, tense with apprehension. As the noise dies off, he seems to relax, but the alert hunted look is still in his eyes which are ringed in a reddish color. The rest of his body has been whitened with a floury substance. He is naked down to the waist, wears a baggy pair of trousers, calf-length, and around both feet are bangles.*)

EMAN. I will simply stay here till dawn. I have done enough. (*A window is thrown open and a woman empties some slop from a pail. With a startled cry Eman leaps aside to avoid it and the woman puts out her head.*)

WOMAN. Oh, my head. What have I done! Eh, it's the carrier! (*Very rapidly she clears her throat and spits on him, flings the pail at him and runs off, shouting.*) He's here. The carrier is hiding in the passage. Quickly, I have found the carrier! (*The cry is taken up and Eman flees down the passage. Shortly afterwards his pursuers come pouring down the passage in full cry. After the last of them come Jaguna and Oroge.*)

OROGE. Wait, wait. I cannot go so fast.

JAGUNA. We will rest a little then. We can do nothing anyway.

OROGE. If only he had let me prepare him.

JAGUNA. They are the ones who break first, these fools who think they were born to carry suffering like a hat. What are we to do now?

OROGE. When they catch him I must prepare him.

JAGUNA. He? It will be impossible now. There can be no joy left in that one.

OROGE. Still, it took him by surprise. He was not expecting what he met.

JAGUNA. Why then did he refuse to listen? Did he think he was coming to sit down to a feast? He had not even gone through one compound before he bolted. Did he think he was taken round the people to be blessed? A woman, that is all he is.

OROGE. No, no. He took the beating well enough. I think he is the kind who would let himself be beaten from night till dawn and

52

not utter a sound. He would let himself be stoned until he dropped dead.

JAGUNA. Then what made him run like a coward?

OROGE. I don't know. I don't really know. It is a night of curses Jaguna. It is not many unprepared minds will remain unhinged under the load.

JAGUNA. We must find him. It is poor beginning for a year when our own curses remain hovering over our homes because the carrier refused to take them. (*They go. The scene changes. Eman is crouching beside some shrubs, torn and bleeding.*)

EMAN. They are even guarding my house . . . as if I would go there, but I need water . . . they could at least grant me that . . . I can be thirsty too . . . (*He pricks his ears.*) . . . there must be a stream nearby . . . (*As he looks round him, his eyes widen at a scene he encounters. An old man, short and vigorous looking is seated on a stool. He also is wearing calf-length baggy trousers, white. On his head, a white cap. An attendant is engaged in rubbing his body with oil. Round eyes, two white rings have already been marked.*)

OLD MAN. Have they prepared the boat?

ATTENDANT. They are making the last sacrifice.

OLD MAN. Good. Did you send for my son?

ATTENDANT. He is on his way.

OLD MAN. I have never met the carrying of the boat with such a heavy heart. I hope nothing comes of it.

ATTENDANT. The gods will not desert us on that account.

OLD MAN. A man should be at his strongest when he takes the boat my friend. To be weighed down inside and out is not a wise thing. I hope when the moment comes I shall have found my strength. (*Enter Eman, a wrapper round his waist and a "dansiki" over it.*) I meant to wait until after my journey to the river, but my mind is so burdened with my own grief and yours I could not delay it. You know I must have all my strength. But I sit here, feeling it all eat slowly away by my unspoken grief. It helps to say it out. It even helps to cry sometimes. (*He signals to the attendant to leave them.*) Come nearer . . . we will never meet again, son. Not on this side of the flesh. What I do not know is whether you will return to take my place.

EMAN. I will never come back.

OLD MAN. Do you know what you are saying? Ours is a strong

53

breed my son. It is only a strong breed that can take this boat to the river year after year and wax stronger on it. I have taken down each year's evils for over twenty years. I hoped you would follow me.

EMAN. My life here died with Omae.

OLD MAN. Your wife died giving birth to your child and you think the world is ended. Eman, my pain did not begin when Omae died. Since you sent her to stay with me, son, I lived with the burden of knowing that this child would die bearing your son.

EMAN. Father . . .

OLD MAN. Don't you know it was the same with you? You killed your mother. She died giving birth to you. Son, it is not the mouth of the boaster that says he belongs to the strong breed. It is the tongue that is red with pain and black with sorrow. Twelve years you were away my son, and for those twelve years I knew the love of an old man for his daughter and the pain of a man helplessly awaiting his loss.

EMAN. I wish I had stayed away. I wish I never came back to meet her.

OLD MAN. It had to be. But you know now what slowly ate away my strength. I awaited your return with love and fear. Forgive me then if I say that your grief is light. It will pass. This grief may drive you now from home. But you must return.

EMAN. You do not understand. It is not grief alone.

OLD MAN. What is it then? Tell me, I can still learn.

EMAN. I was away twelve years. I changed much in that time.

OLD MAN. I am listening.

EMAN. I am unfitted for your work father. I wish to say no more. But I am totally unfitted for your call.

OLD MAN. It is only time you need son. Stay longer and you will answer the urge of your blood.

EMAN. That I stayed at all was because of Omae. I did not expect to find her waiting. I would have taken her away, but strong breed though you are father, it would have killed you. And I was a tired man. I needed peace. Because Omae was peace, I stayed. Now nothing holds me here.

OLD MAN. Other men would rot and die doing this task year after year. It is strong medicine which only we can take. Our blood is strong like no other. Anything you do in life must be less than this, son.

EMAN. That is not true father.

OLD MAN. I tell you it is true. Your own blood will betray you, son. Because you cannot hold it back. If you make it do less than this, it will rush to your head and burst it open. I say what I know my son.

EMAN. There are other tasks in life father. This one is not for me. There are even greater things you know nothing of.

OLD MAN. I am very sad. You only go to give to others what rightly belongs to us. You will use your strength among thieves. They are thieves because they take what is ours, they have no claim of blood to it. They will even lack the knowledge to use it wisely. Truth is my companion at this moment my son. I know everything I say will surely bring the sadness of truth.

EMAN. I am going father.

OLD MAN. Call my attendant. And be with me in your strength for this last journey. A-ah, did you hear that? It came out without my knowing it; this is indeed my last journey. But I am not afraid. (*Eman goes out. A few moments later, the attendant enters.*)

ATTENDANT. The boat is ready.

OLD MAN. So am I. (*He sits perfectly still for several moments. Drumming begins somewhere in the distance, and the old man sways his head almost imperceptibly. Two men come in bearing a miniature boat, containing an indefinable mound. They rush it in and set it briskly down near the old man, and stand well back. The old man gets up slowly, the attendant watching him keenly. He signs to the men, who lift the boat quickly onto the old man's head. As soon as it touches his head, he holds it down with both hands and runs off, the men give him a start, then follow at a trot. As the last man disappears Oroge limps in and comes face to face with Eman—as carrier—who is now seen still standing beside the shrubs, staring into the scene he has just witnessed. Oroge, struck by the look on Eman's face, looks anxiously behind him to see what has engaged Eman's attention. Eman notices him then, and the pair stare at each other. Jaguna enters, sees him and shouts, "Here he is," rushes at Eman who is whipped back to reality and flees, Jaguna in pursuit. Three or four others enter and follow them. Oroge remains where he is, thoughtful.*)

JAGUNA. (*Re-enters.*) They have closed in on him now, we'll get him this time.

OROGE. It is nearly midnight.

55

JAGUNA. You were standing there looking at him as if he was some strange spirit. Why didn't you shout?

OROGE. You shouted, didn't you? Did that catch him?

JAGUNA. Don't worry. We have him now. But things have taken a bad turn. It is no longer enough to drive him past every house. There is too much contamination about already.

OROGE. (Not listening.) He saw something. Why may I not know what it was?

JAGUNA. What are you talking about?

OROGE. Hm. What is it?

JAGUNA. I said there is too much harm done already. The year will demand more from this carrier than we thought.

OROGE. What do you mean?

JAGUNA. Do we have to talk with the full mouth?

OROGE. S-sh . . . look! (Jaguna turns just in time to see Sunma fly at him, clawing at his face like a crazed tigress.)

SUNMA. Murderer! What are you doing to him? Murderer! Murderer! (Jaguna finds himself struggling really hard to keep off his daughter, he succeeds in pushing her off and striking her so hard on the face that she falls to her knees. He moves on her to hit her again.)

OROGE. (Comes between.) Think what you are doing Jaguna, she is your daughter.

JAGUNA. My daughter! Does this one look like my daughter? Let me cripple the harlot for life.

OROGE. That is a wicked thought Jaguna.

JAGUNA. Don't come between me and her.

OROGE. Nothing in anger—do you forget what tonight is?

JAGUNA. Can you blame me for forgetting? (Draws his hand across his cheek—it is covered with blood.)

OROGE. This is an unhappy night for us all. I fear what is to come of it.

JAGUNA. Let us go. I cannot restrain myself in this creature's presence. My own daughter . . . and for a stranger . . . (They go off. Ifada, who came in with Sunma and had stood apart, horror-stricken, comes shyly forward. He helps Sunma up. They go off, he holding Sunma bent and sobbing. Enter Eman—as carrier. He is physically present in the bounds of this next scene, a side of a round thatched hut. A young girl, about sixteen runs in, stops *beside the hut. She looks round carefully to see that she is not observed, puts her mouth to a little hole in the wall.*)

OMAE. Eman . . . Eman . . . (*Eman—as carrier—responds, as he does throughout the scene, but they are unaware of him.*)

EMAN. (*From inside.*) Who is it?

OMAE. It is me, Omae.

EMAN. How dare you come here! (*Two hands appear at the hole and pushing outwards, create a much larger hole through which Eman puts out his head. It is Eman as a boy, the same age as the girl.*) Go away at once. Are you trying to get me into trouble?

OMAE. What is the matter?

EMAN. You. Go way.

EMAN. But I came to see you.

EMAN. Are you deaf? I say I do not want to see you. Now go before my tutor catches you.

OMAE. All right. Come out.

EMAN. Do what!

OMAE. Come out.

EMAN. You must be mad.

OMAE. (*Sits on the ground.*) All right, if you don't come out I shall simply stay here until your tutor arrives.

EMAN. (*About to explode, thinks better of it and the head disappears. A moment later he emerges from behind the hut.*) What sort of a devil has got into you?

OMAE. None. I just wanted to see you.

EMAN. (*His mimicry is nearly hysterical.*) None. I just wanted to see you. Do you think this place is the stream where you can go and molest innocent people?

OMAE. (*Coyly.*) Aren't you glad to see me?

EMAN. I am not.

OMAE. Why?

EMAN. Why? Do you really ask me why? Because you are a woman and a most troublesome woman. Don't you know anything about this at all? We are not meant to see any woman. So go away before more harm is done.

OMAE. (*Flirtatious.*) What is so secret about it anyway? What do they teach you?

EMAN. Nothing any woman can understand.

OMAE. Ha ha. You think we don't know eh? You've all come to be circumcised.

EMAN. Shut up. You don't know anything.

OMAE. Just think, all this time you haven't been circumcised, and you dared make eyes at us women.

EMAN. Thank you—woman. Now go.

OMAE. Do they give you enough to eat?

EMAN. (*Testily.*) No. We are so hungry that when silly girls like you turn up, we eat them.

OMAE. (*Feigning tears.*) Oh, oh, oh, now he's abusing me. He's abusing me.

EMAN. (*Alarmed.*) Don't try that here. Go quickly if you are going to cry.

OMAE. All right, I won't cry.

EMAN. Cry or no cry, go away and leave me alone. What do you think will happen if my tutor turns up now?

OMAE. He won't.

EMAN. (*Mimicking.*) He won't. I suppose you are his wife and he tells you where he goes. In fact this is just the time he comes round to our huts. He could be at the next hut this very moment.

OMAE. Ha ha. You're lying. I left him by the stream, pinching the girls' bottoms. Is that the sort of thing he teaches you?

EMAN. Don't say anything against him or I shall beat you. Isn't it you loose girls who tease him, wiggling your bottoms under his nose?

OMAE. (*Going tearful again.*) A-ah, so I am one of the loose girls eh?

EMAN. Now don't start accusing me of things I did not say.

OMAE. But you said it. You said it.

EMAN. I didn't. Look Omae, someone will hear you and I'll be in disgrace. Why don't you go before anything happens?

OMAE. It's all right. My friends have promised to hold your old rascal tutor till I get back.

EMAN. Then you go back right now. I have work to do. (*Going in.*)

OMAE. (*Runs after and tries to hold him. Eman leaps back, genuinely scared.*) What is the matter? I was not going to bite you.

EMAN. Do you know what you nearly did? You almost touched me!

OMAE. Well?

EMAN. Well! Isn't it enough that you let me set my eyes on you?

58

Must you now totally pollute me with your touch? Don't you understand anything?

OMAE. Oh, that.

EMAN. (*Nearly screaming.*) It is not oh that. Do you think this is only a joke or a little visit like spending the night with your grandmother? This is an important period of my life. Look, these huts, we built them with our own hands. Every boy builds his own. We learn things, do you understand? And we spend much time just thinking. At least, I do. It is the first time I have had nothing to do except think. Don't you see, I am becoming a man. For the first time, I understand that I have a life to fulfil. Has that thought ever worried you?

OMAE. You are frightening me.

EMAN. There. That is all you can say. And what use will that be when a man finds himself alone—like that? (*Points to the hut.*) A man must go on his own, go where no one can help him, and test his strength. Because he may find himself one day sitting alone in a wall as round as that. In there, my mind could hold no other thought. I may never have such moments again to myself. Don't dare to come and steal any more of it.

OMAE. (*This time, genuinely tearful.*) Oh, I know you hate me. You only want to drive me away.

EMAN. (*Impatiently.*) Yes, yes, I know I hate you—but go.

OMAE. (*Going, all tears. Wipes her eyes, suddenly all mischief.*) Eman.

EMAN. What now?

OMAE. I only want to ask one thing . . . do you promise to tell me?

EMAN. Well, what is it?

OMAE. (*Gleefully.*) Does it hurt? (*She turns instantly and flees, landing straight into the arms of the returning tutor.*)

TUTOR. Te-he-he . . . what have we here? What little mouse leaps straight into the beak of the wise old owl, eh? (*Omae struggles to free herself, flies to the opposite side, grimacing with distaste.*) I suppose you merely came to pick some fruits, eh? You did not sneak here to see any of my children.

OMAE. Yes, I came to steal your fruit.

TUTOR. Te-he-he . . . I thought so. And that dutiful son of mine over there. He saw you and came to chase you off my fruit trees, didn't he? Te-he-he . . . I'm sure he did, isn't that so, my young Eman?

EMAN. I was talking to her.

TUTOR. Indeed you were. Now be good enough to go into your hut until I decide your punishment. (*Eman withdraws.*) Te-he-he . . . now now, my little daughter, you need not be afraid of me.

OMAE. (*Spiritedly.*) I am not.

TUTOR. Good. Very good. We ought to be friendly. (*His voice becomes leering.*) Now this is nothing to worry you, my daughter . . . a very small thing indeed. Although of course if I were to let it slip that our young Eman had broken a strong taboo, it might go hard on him, you know. I am sure you would not like that to happen, would you?

OMAE. No.

TUTOR. Good. You are sensible, my girl. Can you wash clothes?

OMAE. Yes.

TUTOR. Good. If you will come with me now to my hut, I shall give you some clothes to wash, and then we will forget all about this matter, eh? Well, come on.

OMAE. I shall wait here. You go and bring the clothes.

TUTOR. Eh? What is that? Now now, don't make me angry. You should know better than to talk back at your elders. Come now. (*He takes her by the arm, and tries to drag her off.*)

OMAE. No, no, I won't come to your hut. Leave me. Leave me alone, you shameless old man.

TUTOR. If you don't come I shall disgrace the whole family of Eman, and yours too. (*Eman re-enters with a small bundle.*)

EMAN. Leave her alone. Let us go, Omae.

TUTOR. And where do you think you are going?

EMAN. Home.

TUTOR. Te-he-he . . . as easy as that, eh? You think you can leave here any time you please? Get right back inside that hut! (*Eman takes Omae by the arm and begins to walk off.*) Come back at once. (*He goes after him and raises his stick. Eman catches it, wrenches it from him and throws it away.*)

OMAE. (*Hopping delightedly.*) Kill him. Beat him to death.

TUTOR. Help! Help! He is killing me! Help! (*Alarmed, Eman clamps his hand over his mouth.*)

EMAN. Old tutor, I don't mean you any harm, but you must not try to harm me either. (*He removes his hand.*)

TUTOR. You think you can get away with your crime. My report shall reach the elders before you ever get into town.

EMAN. You are afraid of what I will say about you? Don't worry. Only if you try to shame me, then I will speak. I am not going back to the village anyway. Just tell them I have gone, no more. If you say one word more than that I shall hear of it the same day and I shall come back.

TUTOR. You are telling me what to do? But don't think to come back next year because I will drive you away. Don't think to come back here even ten years from now. And don't send your children. (*Goes off with threatening gestures.*)

EMAN. I won't come back.

OMAE. Smoked vulture! But, Eman, he says you cannot return next year. What will you do?

EMAN. It is a small thing one can do in the big towns.

OMAE. I thought you were going to beat him that time. Why didn't you crack his dirty hide?

EMAN. Listen carefully, Omae . . . I am going on a journey.

OMAE. Come on. Tell me about it on the way.

EMAN. No, I go that way. I cannot return to the village.

OMAE. Because of that wretched man? Anyway you will first talk to your father.

EMAN. Go and see him for me. Tell him I have gone away for some time. I think he will know.

OMAE. But, Eman . . .

EMAN. I have not finished. You will go and live with him till I get back. I have spoken to him about you. Look after him!

OMAE. But what is this journey? When will you come back?

EMAN. I don't know. But this is a good moment to go. Nothing ties me down.

OMAE. But, Eman, you want to leave me.

EMAN. Don't forget all I said. I don't know how long I will be. Stay in my father's house as long as you remember me. When you become tired of waiting, you must do as you please. You understand? You must do as you please.

OMAE. I cannot understand anything, Eman. I don't know where you are going or why. Suppose you never came back! Don't go, Eman. Don't leave me by myself.

EMAN. I must go. Now let me see you on your way.

OMAE. I shall come with you.

61

EMAN. Come with me! And who will look after you? Me? You will only be in my way, you know that! You would hold me back and I shall desert you in a strange place. Go home and do as I say. Take care of my father and let him take care of you. (*He starts going but Omae clings to him.*)

OMAE. But, Eman, stay the night at least. You will only lose your way. Your father, Eman, what will he say? I won't remember what you said . . . come back to the village . . . I cannot return alone, Eman . . . come with me as far as the crossroads. (*His face set, Eman strides off and Omae loses balance as he increases his pace. Falling, she quickly wraps her arms around his ankle, but Eman continues unchecked, dragging her along.*) Don't go, Eman . . . Eman, don't leave me, don't leave me . . . don't leave your Omae . . . don't go, Eman . . . don't leave your Omae . . . (*Eman— as carrier—makes a nervous move as if he intends to go after the vanished pair. He stops but continues to stare at the point where he last saw them. There is stillness for a while. Then the girl enters from the same place and remains looking at Eman. Startled, Eman looks apprehensively round him. The girl goes nearer but keeps beyond arm's length.*)

GIRL. Are you the carrier?

EMAN. Yes. I am Eman.

GIRL. Why are you hiding?

EMAN. I really came for a drink of water . . . er . . . is there anyone in front of the house?

GIRL. No.

EMAN. But there might be people in the house. Did you hear voices?

GIRL. There is no one there.

EMAN. Good. Thank you. (*He is about to go, stops suddenly.*) Er . . . would you . . . you will find a cup on the table. Could you bring me the water out here? The water-pot is in a corner. (*The girl goes. She enters the house, then, watching Eman carefully, slips out and runs off. Eman, sitting:*) Perhaps they have all gone home. It will be good to rest. (*He hears voices and listens hard.*) Too late. (*Moves cautiously nearer the house.*) Quickly, girl, I can hear people coming. Hurry up. (*Looks through the window.*) Where are you? Where is she? (*The truth dawns on him suddenly and he moves off, sadly. Enter Jaguna and Oroge, led by the girl.*)

GIRL. (*Pointing.*) He was there.

JAGUNA. Ay, he's gone now. He is a sly one is your friend. But it won't save him for ever.

OROGE. What was he doing when you saw him?

GIRL. He asked me for a drink of water.

JAGUNA and OROGE. Ah! (*They look at each other.*)

OROGE. We should have thought of that.

JAGUNA. He is surely finished now. If only we had thought of it earlier.

OROGE. It is not too late. There is still an hour before midnight.

JAGUNA. We must call back all the men. Now we need only wait for him—in the right place.

OROGE. Everyone must be told. We don't want anyone heading him off again.

JAGUNA. And it works so well. This is surely the help of the gods themselves, Oroge. Don't you know at once what is on the path to the stream?

OROGE. The sacred trees.

JAGUNA. I tell you it is the very hand of the gods. Let us go. (*An overgrown part of the village. Eman wanders in, aimlessly, seemingly uncaring of discovery. Beyond him an area lights up, revealing a group of people clustered round a spot, all the heads are bowed. One figure stands away and separate from them. Even as Eman looks, the group break up and the people disperse, coming down and past him. Only three people are left, a man whose back is turned, the village priest and the isolated one. They stand on opposite sides of the grave, the man on the mound of earth. The priest walks round to the man's side and lays a hand on his shoulder.*)

PRIEST. Come.

EMAN. I will. Give me a few moments here alone.

PRIEST. Be comforted. (*They fall silent.*)

EMAN. I was gone twelve years but she waited. She whom I thought had too much of the laughing child in her. Twelve years I was a pilgrim, seeking the vain shrine of secret strength. And all the time, strange knowledge, this silent strength of my child-woman.

PRIEST. We all saw it. It was a lesson to us; we did not know that such goodness could be found among us.

EMAN. Then why? Why the wasted years if she had to perish

63

giving birth to my child? (*They are both silent.*) I do not really know for what great meaning I searched. When I returned, I could not be certain I had found it. Until I reached my home and I found her a full-grown woman, still a child at heart. When I grew to believe it, I thought, this, after all, is what I sought. It was here all the time. And I threw away my new-gained knowledge. I buried the part of me that was formed in strange places. I made a home in my birth-place.

PRIEST. That was as it should be.

EMAN. Any truth of that was killed in the cruelty of her brief happiness.

PRIEST. (*Looks up and sees the figure standing away from them, the child in his arms. He is totally still.*) Your father—he is over there.

EMAN. I knew he would come. Has he my son with him?

PRIEST. Yes.

EMAN. He will let no one take the child. Go and comfort him, priest. He loved Omae like a daughter, and you all know how well she looked after him. You see how strong we really are. In his heart of hearts the old man's love really awaited a daughter. Go and comfort him. His grief is more than mine. (*The priest goes. The old man has stood well away from the burial group. His face is hard and his gaze unswerving from the grave. The priest goes to him, pauses, but sees that he can make no dent in the man's grief. Bowed, he goes on his way. Eman, as carrier, walks towards the graveside, the other Eman having gone. His feet sink into the mound and he breaks slowly onto his knees, scooping up the sand in his hands and pouring it onto his head. The scene blacks out slowly. Enter Jaguna and Oroge.*)

OROGE. We have only a little time.

JAGUNA. He will come. All the wells are guarded. There is only the stream left him. The animal must come to drink.

OROGE. You are sure it will not fail—the trap I mean.

JAGUNA. When Jaguna sets the trap, even elephants pay homage —their trunks downwards and one leg up in the sky. When the carrier steps on the fallen twigs, it is up in the sacred trees with him.

OROGE. I shall breathe again when this long night is over. (*They go out. Enter Eman—as carrier—from the same direction as the*

64

last two entered. In front of him is a still figure, the Old Man as he was carrying the dwarf boat.)

EMAN. (Joyfully.) Father. (The figure does not turn around.) It is your son. Eman. (He moves nearer.) Don't you want to look at me? It is I, Eman. (He moves nearer still.)

OLD MAN. You are coming too close. Don't you know what I carry on my head?

EMAN. But, Father, I am your son.

OLD MAN. Then go back. There cannot be two of us.

EMAN. Tell me first where you are going.

OLD MAN. Do you ask that? Where else but to the river?

EMAN. (Visibly relieved.) I only wanted to be sure. My throat is burning. I have been looking for the stream all night.

OLD MAN. It is the other way.

EMAN. But you said . . .

OLD MAN. I take the longer way, you know I must do this. It is quicker if you take the other way. Go now.

EMAN. No, I will only get lost again. I shall go with you.

OLD MAN. Go back, my son. Go back.

EMAN. Why? Won't you even look at me?

OLD MAN. Listen to your father. Go back.

EMAN. But, Father! (He makes to hold him. Instantly the old man breaks into a rapid trot. Eman hesitates, then follows, his strength nearly gone.) Wait, Father. I am coming with you . . . wait . . . wait for me, Father . . . (There is a sound of twigs breaking, of a sudden trembling in the branches. Then silence. The front of Eman's house. The effigy is hanging from the sheaves. Enter Sunma, still supported by Ifada. She stands transfixed as she sees the hanging figure. Ifada appears to go mad, rushes at the object and tears it down. Sunma, her last bit of will gone, crumbles against the wall. Some distance away from them, partly hidden, stands the girl, impassively watching. Ifada hugs the effigy to him, stands above Sunma. The girl remains where she is, observing. Almost at once, the villagers begin to return, subdued and guilty. They walk across the front, skirting the house as widely as they can. No word is exchanged. Jaguna and Oroge eventually appear. Jaguna who is leading, sees Sunma as soon as he comes in view. He stops at once, retreating slightly.)

OROGE. (Almost whispering.) What is it?

JAGUNA. The viper. (Oroge looks cautiously at the woman.)

OROGE. I don't think she will even see you.

JAGUNA. Are you sure? I am in no frame of mind for another meeting with her.

OROGE. Let us go home.

JAGUNA. I am sick to the heart of the cowardice I have seen tonight.

OROGE. That is the nature of men.

JAGUNA. Then it is a sorry world to live in. We did it for them. It was all for their own common good. What did it benefit me whether the man lived or died? But did you see them? One and all they looked up at the man and words died in their throats.

OROGE. It was no common sight.

JAGUNA. Women could not have behaved so shamefully. One by one they crept off like sick dogs. Not one could raise a curse.

OROGE. It was not only him they fled. Do you see how unattended we are?

JAGUNA. There are those who will pay for this night's work!

OROGE. Ay, let us go home. (*They go off. Sunma, Ifada, and the girl remain as they are, the light fading slowly on them.*)

THE END

PROPERTY PLOT

On Stage (in hut):
   Table, with medical gear
   Cupboard
   Table, with textbooks and exercise books
   Buba (native garment), on wall
   Large stick
   "Ayo" board, with seeds, on shelf
   Stools (2)

Off Stage:
   Small raffia sack (Man Traveller)
   Cloth-covered basket (Woman Traveller)
   Basket of oranges (Ifada)
   Effigy ("carrier") with rope attached to leg (Girl)
   Large sack
   Kerosene lamps (2) (inner part of hut)
   Torch
   Pail, with slops (behind window)
   Stool, for old man
   Rubbing oil (Attendant)
   Miniature boat and mound of sand
   Small bundle (Eman)
   Stick (Tutor)

NOTE: costumes should be colorful African style, as in "The Trials of Brother Jero."

NEW PLAYS

★ **THE EXONERATED by Jessica Blank and Erik Jensen.** Six interwoven stories paint a picture of an American criminal justice system gone horribly wrong and six brave souls who persevered to survive it. "The #1 play of the year...intense and deeply affecting..." *–NY Times.* "Riveting. Simple, honest storytelling that demands reflection." *–A.P.* "Artful and moving...pays tribute to the resilience of human hearts and minds." *–Variety.* "Stark...riveting...cunningly orchestrated." *–The New Yorker.* "Hard-hitting, powerful, and socially relevant." *–Hollywood Reporter.* [7M, 3W] ISBN: 0-8222-1946-8

★ **STRING FEVER by Jacquelyn Reingold.** Lily juggles the big issues: turning forty, artificial insemination and the elusive scientific Theory of Everything in this Off-Broadway comedy hit. "Applies the elusive rules of string theory to the conundrums of one woman's love life. Think *Sex and the City* meets *Copenhagen*." *–NY Times.* "A funny offbeat and touching look at relationships...an appealing romantic comedy populated by oddball characters." *–NY Daily News.* "Where kooky, zany, and madcap meet...whimsically winsome." *–NY Magazine.* "STRING FEVER will have audience members happily stringing along." *–TheaterMania.com.* "Reingold's language is surprising, inventive, and unique." *–nytheatre.com.* "...[a] whimsical comic voice." *–Time Out.* [3M, 3W (doubling)] ISBN: 0-8222-1952-2

★ **DEBBIE DOES DALLAS adapted by Erica Schmidt, composed by Andrew Sherman, conceived by Susan L. Schwartz.** A modern morality tale told as a comic musical of tragic proportions as the classic film is brought to the stage. "A scream! A saucy, tongue-in-cheek romp." *–The New Yorker.* "Hilarious! DEBBIE manages to have it all: beauty, brains and a great sense of humor!" *–Time Out.* "Shamelessly silly, shrewdly self-aware and proud of being naughty. Great fun!" *–NY Times.* "Racy and raucous, a lighthearted, fast-paced thoroughly engaging and hilarious send-up." *–NY Daily News.* [3M, 5W] ISBN: 0-8222-1955-7

★ **THE MYSTERY PLAYS by Roberto Aguirre-Sacasa.** Two interrelated one acts, loosely based on the tradition of the medieval mystery plays. "... stylish, spine-tingling...Mr. Aguirre-Sacasa uses standard tricks of horror stories, borrowing liberally from masters like Kafka, Lovecraft, Hitchcock...But his mastery of the genre is his own...irresistible." *–NY Times.* "Undaunted by the special-effects limitations of theatre, playwright and *Marvel* comic-book writer Roberto Aguirre-Sacasa maps out some creepy twilight zones in THE MYSTERY PLAYS, an engaging, related pair of one acts...The theatre may rarely deliver shocks equivalent to, say, *Dawn of the Dead*, but Aguirre-Sacasa's work is fine compensation." *–Time Out.* [4M, 2W] ISBN: 0-8222-2038-5

★ **THE JOURNALS OF MIHAIL SEBASTIAN by David Auburn.** This epic one-man play spans eight tumultuous years and opens a uniquely personal window on the Romanian Holocaust and the Second World War. "Powerful." *–NY Times.* "[THE JOURNALS OF MIHAIL SEBASTIAN] allows us to glimpse the idiosyncratic effects of that awful history on one intelligent, pragmatic, recognizably real man..." *–NY Newsday.* [3M, 5W] ISBN: 0-8222-2006-7

★ **LIVING OUT by Lisa Loomer.** The story of the complicated relationship between a Salvadoran nanny and the Anglo lawyer she works for. "A stellar new play. Searingly funny." *–The New Yorker.* "Both generous and merciless, equally enjoyable and disturbing." *–NY Newsday.* "A bitingly funny new comedy. The plight of working mothers is explored from two pointedly contrasting perspectives in this sympathetic, sensitive new play." *–Variety.* [2M, 6W] ISBN: 0-8222-1994-8

DRAMATISTS PLAY SERVICE, INC.
440 Park Avenue South, New York, NY 10016 212-683-8960 Fax 212-213-1539
postmaster@dramatists.com www.dramatists.com

NEW PLAYS

★ **MATCH by Stephen Belber.** Mike and Lisa Davis interview a dancer and choreographer about his life, but it is soon evident that their agenda will either ruin or inspire them—and definitely change their lives forever. "Prolific laughs and ear-to-ear smiles." —*NY Magazine.* "Uproariously funny, deeply moving, enthralling theater. Stephen Belber's MATCH has great beauty and tenderness, and abounds in wit." —*NY Daily News.* "Three and a half out of four stars." —*USA Today.* "A theatrical steeplechase that leads straight from outrageous bitchery to unadorned, heartfelt emotion." —*Wall Street Journal.* [2M, 1W] ISBN: 0-8222-2020-2

★ **HANK WILLIAMS: LOST HIGHWAY by Randal Myler and Mark Harelik.** The story of the beloved and volatile country-music legend Hank Williams, featuring twenty-five of his most unforgettable songs. "[LOST HIGHWAY has] the exhilarating feeling of Williams on stage in a particular place on a particular night...serves up classic country with the edges raw and the energy hot...By the end of the play, you've traveled on a profound emotional journey: LOST HIGHWAY transports its audience and communicates the inspiring message of the beauty and richness of Williams' songs...forceful, clear-eyed, moving, impressive." —*Rolling Stone.* "...honors a very particular musical talent with care and energy... smart, sweet, poignant." —*NY Times.* [7M, 3W] ISBN: 0-8222-1985-9

★ **THE STORY by Tracey Scott Wilson.** An ambitious black newspaper reporter goes against her editor to investigate a murder and finds the *best* story...but at what cost? "A singular new voice...deeply emotional, deeply intellectual, and deeply musical..." —*The New Yorker.* "...a conscientious and absorbing new drama..." —*NY Times.* "...a riveting, tough-minded drama about race, reporting and the truth..." —*A.P.* "... a stylish, attention-holding script that ends on a chilling note that will leave viewers with much to talk about." —*Curtain Up.* [2M, 7W (doubling, flexible casting)] ISBN: 0-8222-1998-0

★ **OUR LADY OF 121st STREET by Stephen Adly Guirgis.** The body of Sister Rose, beloved Harlem nun, has been stolen, reuniting a group of life-challenged childhood friends who square off as they wait for her return. "A scorching and dark new comedy... Mr. Guirgis has one of the finest imaginations for dialogue to come along in years." —*NY Times.* "Stephen Guirgis may be the best playwright in America under forty." —*NY Magazine.* [8M, 4W] ISBN: 0-8222-1965-4

★ **HOLLYWOOD ARMS by Carrie Hamilton and Carol Burnett.** The coming-of-age story of a dreamer who manages to escape her bleak life and follow her romantic ambitions to stardom. Based on Carol Burnett's bestselling autobiography, *One More Time.* "...pure theatre and pure entertainment..." —*Talkin' Broadway.* "...a warm, fuzzy evening of theatre." —*BrodwayBeat.com.* "...chuckles and smiles of recognition or surprise flow naturally...a remarkable slice of life." —*TheatreScene.net.* [5M, 5W, 1 girl] ISBN: 0-8222-1959-X

★ **INVENTING VAN GOGH by Steven Dietz.** A haunting and hallucinatory drama about the making of art, the obsession to create and the fine line that separates truth from myth. "Like a van Gogh painting, Dietz's story is a gorgeous example of excess—one that remakes reality with broad, well-chosen brush strokes. At evening's end, we're left with the author's resounding opinions on art and artifice, and provoked by his constant query into which is greater: van Gogh's art or his violent myth." —*Phoenix New Times.* "Dietz's writing is never simple. It is always brilliant. Shaded, compressed, direct, lucid—he frames his subject with a remarkable understanding of painting as a physical experience." —*Tucson Citizen.* [4M, 1W] ISBN: 0-8222-1954-9

DRAMATISTS PLAY SERVICE, INC.
440 Park Avenue South, New York, NY 10016 212-683-8960 Fax 212-213-1539
postmaster@dramatists.com www.dramatists.com

NEW PLAYS

★ **INTIMATE APPAREL by Lynn Nottage.** The moving and lyrical story of a turn-of-the-century black seamstress whose gifted hands and sewing machine are the tools she uses to fashion her dreams from the whole cloth of her life's experiences. "…Nottage's play has a delicacy and eloquence that seem absolutely right for the time she is depicting…" –*NY Daily News*. "…thoughtful, affecting…The play offers poignant commentary on an era when the cut and color of one's dress—and of course, skin—determined whom one could and could not marry, sleep with, even talk to in public." –*Variety*. [2M, 4W] ISBN: 0-8222-2009-1

★ **BROOKLYN BOY by Donald Margulies.** A witty and insightful look at what happens to a writer when his novel hits the bestseller list. "The characters are beautifully drawn, the dialogue sparkles…" –*nytheatre.com*. "Few playwrights have the mastery to smartly investigate so much through a laugh-out-loud comedy that combines the vintage subject matter of successful writer-returning-to-ethnic-roots with the familiar mid-life crisis." –*Show Business Weekly*. [4M, 3W] ISBN: 0-8222-2074-1

★ **CROWNS by Regina Taylor.** Hats become a springboard for an exploration of black history and identity in this celebratory musical play. "Taylor pulls off a Hat Trick: She scores thrice, turning CROWNS into an artful amalgamation of oral history, fashion show, and musical theater…" –*TheatreMania.com*. "…wholly theatrical…Ms. Taylor has created a show that seems to arise out of spontaneous combustion, as if a bevy of department-store customers simultaneously decided to stage a revival meeting in the changing room." –*NY Times*. [1M, 6W (2 musicians)] ISBN: 0-8222-1963-8

★ **EXITS AND ENTRANCES by Athol Fugard.** The story of a relationship between a young playwright on the threshold of his career and an aging actor who has reached the end of his. "[Fugard] can say more with a single line than most playwrights convey in an entire script…Paraphrasing the title, it's safe to say this drama, making its memorable entrance into our consciousness, is unlikely to exit as long as a theater exists for exceptional work." –*Variety*. "A thought-provoking, elegant and engrossing new play…" –*Hollywood Reporter*. [2M] ISBN: 0-8222-2041-5

★ **BUG by Tracy Letts.** A thriller featuring a pair of star-crossed lovers in an Oklahoma City motel facing a bug invasion, paranoia, conspiracy theories and twisted psychological motives. "…obscenely exciting…top-flight craftsmanship. Buckle up and brace yourself…" –*NY Times*. "…[a] thoroughly outrageous and thoroughly entertaining play…the possibility of enemies, real and imagined, to squash has never been more theatrical." –*A.P.* [3M, 2W] ISBN: 0-8222-2016-4

★ **THOM PAIN (BASED ON NOTHING) by Will Eno.** An ordinary man muses on childhood, yearning, disappointment and loss, as he draws the audience into his last-ditch plea for empathy and enlightenment. "It's one of those treasured nights in the theater—treasured nights anywhere, for that matter—that can leave you both breathless with exhilaration and…in a puddle of tears." –*NY Times*. "Eno's words…are familiar, but proffered in a way that is constantly contradictory to our expectations. Beckett is certainly among his literary ancestors." –*nytheatre.com*. [1M] ISBN: 0-8222-2076-8

★ **THE LONG CHRISTMAS RIDE HOME by Paula Vogel.** Past, present and future collide on a snowy Christmas Eve for a troubled family of five. "…[a] lovely and hauntingly original family drama…a work that breathes so much life into the theater." –*Time Out*. "…[a] delicate visual feast…" –*NY Times*. "…brutal and lovely…the overall effect is magical." –*NY Newsday*. [3M, 3W] ISBN: 0-8222-2003-2

DRAMATISTS PLAY SERVICE, INC.
440 Park Avenue South, New York, NY 10016 212-683-8960 Fax 212-213-1539
postmaster@dramatists.com www.dramatists.com